31 DAYS of SPIRITUAL GROWTH

In our church, we like to say that books are "missionaries," but books can be "mentors" too! In *31 Days of Spiritual Growth*, Dr. Randy Bozarth has captured the essence of spiritual development—the incremental day-by-day process of "growing up" in Christ. With thirty-one thought-provoking entries, Dr. Bozarth provides a no-nonsense daily "track" for personal growth. Let this book "mentor" you as it pushes the envelope of spiritual maturity and helps you achieve the growth you desire.

—Marilyn Hickey
Founder and President of Marilyn Hickey Ministries

Reading and absorbing *31 Days of Spiritual Growth* will be a worthwhile investment of your time. Get your copy today and share it with others.

—Freda Lindsay
Co-Founder of Christ For The Nations

31 DAYS of SPIRITUAL GROWTH

RANDY BOZARTH

WHITAKER
HOUSE

31 Days of Spiritual Growth:
Discover Your Passionate Purpose

Randy Bozarth
World Missions Advance
PO Box 764408
Dallas TX 75376-4408

ISBN: 978-0-88368-619-5
Printed in the United States of America
© 2007 by Randy Bozarth

Whitaker House
1030 Hunt Valley Circle
New Kensington, PA 15068
www.whitakerhouse.com

Library of Congress Cataloging-in-Publication Data
Bozarth, Randy.
31 days of spiritual growth : discover your passionate purpose / Randy Bozarth.
p.   cm.
Summary: "A thirty-one day devotional that emphasizes the importance of Christian growth and maturity"—Provided by publisher.
Includes bibliographical references and index.
ISBN-13: 978-0-88368-619-5 (trade pbk. : alk. paper)
ISBN-10: 0-88368-619-8 (trade pbk. : alk. paper) 1. Spiritual formation.
2. Devotional calendars. I. Title. II. Title: Thirty-one days of spiritual growth.
BV4511.B695 2007
248.4—dc22   2006039424

No part of this book may be reproduced or transmitted in any form or by any means, electronic or mechanical—including photocopying, recording, or by any information storage and retrieval system—without permission in writing from the publisher. Please direct your inquiries to permissionseditor@whitakerhouse.com.

1 2 3 4 5 6 7 8 9 10 11 12 **LU** 15 14 13 12 11 10 09 08 07

CONTENTS

ACKNOWLEDGMENTS

Knowing how to grow up in the Lord is the most important insight any Christian can embrace in his or her personal relationship with Him. One real way to have the purest growth is by surrounding yourself with people who will point out areas in your life that need to be changed, because of their love and care for you.

In writing this book, all of those people from my past have come to mind. There is no way I can personally list them, thanking each of them. But I want to acknowledge all the friends, pastors, and family members who have encouraged me over the years, speaking so much into my life.

Each of my pastors, every Sunday school teacher, every coach from my days of participation in school sports—all of those who saw gifts of God in me or saw shortcomings and spurred me on to *grow up* and more fully embrace His plan and purposes for my life—thank you!

Through all the seasons of my life, I have been blessed to have these wonderful mentors who taught and encouraged me to further maturity. Each of them share in this effort.

"FOR I DETERMINED NOT TO KNOW ANYTHING AMONG YOU EXCEPT JESUS CHRIST AND HIM CRUCIFIED."
—1 CORINTHIANS 2:2

DEDICATION

I would like to dedicate this book to my parents, Robert and Verle Bozarth. I am so blessed to have been brought up in such a godly home.

My parents were saved—gloriously—in a "Voice of Healing" revival being held in Clinton, Illinois, in December 1950. I was only one-and-a-half years old at that time, so their salvation came early enough in my life for me to enjoy the benefits from my earliest recollections. I grew up in a home where my parents' passion for God and His house were always in the forefront of our family life.

It seemed our family was always one of the first to arrive at church and one of the last to leave. Their commitment was a foundational building block for my life and calling—a heritage I will always appreciate and cherish.

Now in their retirement years, Mom and Dad's passion for God's presence and His Word has not subsided. It continues to shape their day-to-day lives. If anything, their desire for the things of God is stronger than ever before.

Thank you, Mom and Dad, for your holy determination, and for instilling this same desire in me.

INTRODUCTION

I believe that, regardless of our perspective, there is a deep and abiding desire inside each of us to be a fulfilled and mature person before we reach the end of our lives here on earth. I have never met anyone who did not want to finish this "race of life" successfully—going the distance and finishing strong. No Olympic runner competes just to run, but rather to finish the race and finish it strong.

Even a life well lived, one that is taking advantage of all the precious opportunities it is afforded, cannot say, "There is nothing left to achieve." Though you may be able to say, by God's grace and favor working in your life, "I am doing better in life than I ever could have expected," you cannot honestly say, "I have fully arrived."

Perhaps wonderful things have happened, and you are living a fairly comfortable life. Or perhaps you feel your maturity level is high because you have weathered hurtful or despairing tragedies. It is true that trials and tests can bring maturity, and many of us do achieve a great deal of maturity through both the good and bad experiences of life. But I doubt any of us can say, "I have nothing else left to learn."

Each of us has a deep need, which can become a passionate drive when guided by the Lord Himself, to continue in the race. I believe this is a gift of God, a gift of life. I hope this book will help you in your pursuit, particularly as a tool that guides you toward deeper understanding and greater maturity.

I believe it can certainly become that resource for your life if you choose to take the next thirty-one days and allow God to change your heart.

GROWTH INSIGHT

Growing up
in life is not
automatic.
It is a choice!

EVEN JESUS HAD STEPS OF GROWTH

*And the Child grew and became strong
in spirit, filled with wisdom; and the
grace of God was upon Him.*
—Luke 2:40

When the Holy Spirit begins to enlighten you about your need for spiritual growth, it may come as a surprise to you. It seems most Christians today think that just because they have accepted Jesus and have been church members for a long time, they have no need to work on growth. Regular church attendance does not automatically mean that spiritual growth is being produced in our lives. There are deeper issues and commitments each of us has to examine. Let's look at some common issues dealing with Christian maturity in an effort to more readily examine our own lives.

AGE IN GOD'S KINGDOM DOES NOT AUTOMATICALLY EQUAL MATURITY

In the book of Job, we have a powerful confirmation of the truth that extended time spent in God's kingdom does not mean automatic maturity. In chapter 23, we hear a young man named Elihu make a powerful statement. Up to this point, through all of Job's experiences—challenges, confused times, and steps of growth—Elihu remained silent. Perhaps this is because he was younger than Job's three other friends.

In this passage, he was angry with Job's three friends because, though they had not discovered the reason for Job's suffering, they condemned Job nonetheless. Elihu was also angry with Job because of his apparent self-righteousness. Job seemed to be justifying himself rather than allowing God to do so.

Here is what Elihu said about age and wisdom in this important Scripture:

> *Now because they were years older than he, Elihu had waited to speak to Job. When Elihu saw that there was no answer in the mouth of these three men, his wrath was aroused. So Elihu, the son of Barachel the Buzite, answered and said: "I am young in years, and you are very old; therefore I was afraid, and dared not declare my opinion to you. I said, 'Age should speak, and multitude of years should teach wisdom.' But there is a spirit in man, and the breath of the Almighty gives him understanding. Great men are not always wise, nor do the aged always understand justice."* (Job 32:4–9)

Elihu recognized that the older men around him, who should have known more about God, still had significant immaturities—both the friends of Job and Job himself.

Because Job is described at the beginning of his story as a holy, sinless man and is later described affirmatively again in the New Testament (see James 5:11), we see that even great men who know God well can have unknown immaturities in their lives. We can be Christians for many years, living good and consistent Christian lives, but still be very immature in some areas. The challenge, then, is to not become complacent, but rather to actively pursue steps toward further growth and development in particular areas.

The whole key to this Scripture in Job is the issue of spiritual maturity. It does not matter how long you've been a Christian; it is not time or age in God's kingdom that produces maturity in you. When we examine Elihu's response, we see he had insight and revelation important for all of us to grasp: *"But there is a spirit in man, and the breath of the Almighty gives him understanding"* (Job 32:8). The good news is the Holy Spirit does the work! As you continue to take steps of maturity, the Holy Spirit living in you will give you wisdom, strength, passion, and purpose. Another prime example of this principle comes from our Savior Himself.

GROWTH INSIGHT

Neither time nor age produces maturity in you.

ONLY TWO REASONS FOR CHRIST'S LIFE ON EARTH

The first and most important reason Jesus came to earth was to die for our sins and be raised from the dead as the firstfruits of our own eternal life.

> *And as it is appointed for men to die once, but after this the judgment, so Christ was offered once to bear the sins of many. To those who eagerly wait for Him He will appear a second time, apart from sin, for salvation.* (Hebrews 9:27–28)

This doctrine of God as our loving Father who sent His Son to bear the burden of our sin is taught from the very beginning of the Old Testament and continues throughout the New Testament. What joy and freedom it brings to each of us, as believers, when we wake up every morning desiring to serve the Lord in righteousness. Knowing we cannot achieve it even on our very best days, what abiding peace and strength comes when we recognize the redemptive work of our Savior. In Him, we can live righteously every day. That provision for each of us *is* the primary reason Jesus came.

There is, as well, a very important and significant second reason Jesus left His glory in heaven to live on earth for thirty-three years. Have you ever wondered why Jesus did not just come to earth in a UFO, walk around for a few weeks, create a little disturbance with the Roman Empire, and then give His life on the cross? Since it was His sacrifice that paid the price, He could have accomplished our salvation in much less than thirty-three years.

> **GROWTH INSIGHT**
>
> Serving the Lord brings joy and freedom to the believer.

I am sure that would have been a much easier way for Jesus, but He came to earth to fulfill the heart and plan of God—a plan that was conceived even before Adam and Eve were created. God wanted a family (a people) who would desire to be like Him and walk before Him in obedience and maturity. He begins this process in each of us when we repent of our sins and accept Jesus' work on the cross. Our salvation immediately makes us a son or daughter of God. Christ's blood cleanses us and makes us completely right with God, our heavenly Father. It does not, however, make us instantly mature!

I believe the whole reason Jesus came to earth and was born as a natural baby was to be an example to us of how we must walk out our maturity process. Jesus grew up naturally and spiritually, taking new steps of obedience and faith every day of His life on earth. What an example to us of how we can walk out our process of development and find new levels of maturity at every turn and juncture of our everyday lives.

What was Jesus' driving force in taking those daily steps and seeing ever increasing growth and maturity? I believe the answer is a key to our own pursuit of maturity. Jesus wanted desperately to please His heavenly Father and go about doing His business here on earth. The desire of His heart must be our driving force as well. If you are sitting or standing still, you will lose your passion for Christ and no longer add to your maturity. Conversely, as you continue to move forward, the passion in your heart for pleasing God will grow, spurring greater desire for spiritual maturity. Faith's maturity comes through following the Lord every day. In fact, following Him truly means to grow up and begin to experience God's maturity at an ever increasingly deep level in your life.

JESUS, THE HUMBLED AND EXALTED CHRIST

If you exercise regularly for health and fitness as a walker, cyclist, runner, or through another form of exercise, all of your steps in exercising are geared toward achieving strength, endurance, and a sense of development (maturity) toward your goal of having a healthy physical life.

To secure our spiritual health/maturity, Jesus had to take various steps of faith. These first steps are outlined in Paul's writing to the Philippian church, a body of believers he established during his second missionary journey, about AD 51. The story of this church's founding is told in Acts 16:12–40, and in Paul's letter to the Philippians, we learn about Jesus' first steps of faith toward saving mankind.

In this passage, Paul encouraged the Philippians not to continue living in a passive way, but rather to step forward and desire to follow Jesus in a deeper way—becoming more like Jesus Himself. He taught them Jesus' first step, which must also be their first step. Here's the whole passage, and then we'll break it into sections:

> *Let this mind be in you which was also in Christ Jesus, who, being in the form of God, did not consider it robbery to be equal with God, but made Himself of no reputation, taking the form of a bondservant, and coming in the likeness of men. And being found in appearance as a man, He humbled Himself and became obedient to the point of death, even the death of the cross. Therefore God also has highly exalted Him and given Him the name which is above every name, that at the name of Jesus every knee should bow, of those in heaven, and of those on earth, and of those under the earth, and that every tongue should confess that Jesus Christ is Lord, to the glory of God the Father.*
>
> (Philippians 2:5–11)

"Let this mind be in you which was also in Christ Jesus." To take steps of maturity, you have to begin to think like Jesus. Your personal relationship with Jesus requires you to think differently from your corporate relationship with God's people.

"Who, being in the form of God, did not consider it robbery to be equal with God." When Paul referenced the *"form of God,"*

he was not referring to the physical shape of Christ but to His divine essence, a quality that is unchangeable.

"Equal with God" refers to the mode of Christ's existence. Christ shared in the glories and prerogatives of deity but did not regard the circumstances of His existence as something to be jealously retained. He willingly relinquished His glory when He came to earth, yet He retained His deity.

"But made Himself of no reputation, taking the form of a bond-servant, and coming in the likeness of men." The reality of the incarnation is expressed in Christ's complete self-renunciation as He made Himself of no reputation. He veiled the manifestations of deity and assumed real humanity.

"Likeness" suggests that Jesus was really a man, but not merely a man. His humanity was genuine, yet His being was also still divine.

"And being found in appearance as a man, He humbled Himself." Jesus' first step to pleasing His Father God was to leave His glory in heaven and take on the burden of living a totally human life.

> *By this you know the Spirit of God: Every spirit that confesses that Jesus Christ has come in the flesh is of God, and every spirit that does not confess that Jesus Christ has come in the flesh is not of God. And this is the spirit of the Antichrist, which you have heard was coming, and is now already in the world.* (1 John 4:2–3)

We are so often misled, thinking that, because Jesus was the Son of God, He was automatically mature, instantly knowing everything. However, when you begin to understand through the Scripture that Jesus was a man, though not merely a man, you come to some very different conclusions. Again, His humanity was genuine, yet His being was also still divine. Jesus left His glory in heaven to live in this world—spirit, soul, and body. He showed us in "real earthly life" that it is possible, through daily obedience to the Spirit of God, to live a victorious, overcoming, mature life. As Jesus desired to do the will of His Father, He became the supreme example for all of us.

It is important for us not to put more emphasis on the words of Jesus than on the life of Jesus—both are equally important. He was God, so His words are those of God. But His life, lived out in example for us, is important as well; it gives us a picture of God's nature within our earthly realm.

As Jesus dealt with day-to-day disappointments, temptations, and struggles, He did so within His perfect life of maturity, which He had learned through various steps of faith and obedience. Only as He lived a sinless life could His sacrifice on the cross provide the atonement, as the perfect Lamb of God, needed for our perfect forgiveness. And not just forgiveness, but also our ability, by the power of God, to live a growing and victorious, day-to-day, mature life.

> *It came to pass in those days that Jesus came from Nazareth of Galilee, and was baptized by John in the Jordan. And immediately, coming up from the water, He saw the heavens parting and the Spirit descending upon Him like a dove. Then a voice came from heaven, "You are My beloved Son, in whom I am well pleased." Immediately the Spirit drove Him into the wilderness. And He was there in*

the wilderness forty days, tempted by Satan, and was with the wild beasts; and the angels ministered to Him.

(Mark 1:9–13)

This growing, day-to-day maturity in your life comes through daily obedience to the words of our Lord Jesus and through the power of God's Holy Spirit living in you. This is the example given to us through Jesus' life of maturity.

It is important for you to see it was God who led His Son into the wilderness, exposing Him to all manner of temptation. And through Jesus' victory in the wilderness over temptation, we have that same victory and power available to our daily lives.

For we do not have a High Priest who cannot sympathize with our weaknesses, but was in all points tempted as we are, yet without sin. (Hebrews 4:15)

Therefore, in all things He had to be made like His brethren, that He might be a merciful and faithful High Priest in things pertaining to God, to make propitiation for the sins of the people. For in that He Himself has suffered, being tempted, He is able to aid those who are tempted.

(Hebrews 2:17–18)

JESUS, AS A CHILD, GREW NATURALLY AND SPIRITUALLY

From the very beginning of Jesus' natural walk on earth, He developed physically and spiritually through a process of growth. After Jesus' natural parents, Joseph and Mary, took Him to the temple and presented Him to God so that the law of Moses was fulfilled, the Bible says, *"And the Child grew and became strong in spirit, filled with wisdom; and the grace of God was upon Him"* (Luke 2:40).

The Bible reveals to us the continued growth process taking place in Jesus' life a few years later. Joseph and Mary made a yearly trip to Jerusalem for the Feast of the Passover. On one particular trip, Jesus was twelve years old. After the days of the feast were over, His parents returned home, but Jesus stayed behind without Mary and Joseph realizing it. They thought He was somewhere within the group with which they were traveling. After a day's journey, when they realized He was not with any of their relatives or friends, Joseph and Mary returned to Jerusalem to look for Him.

After three days, they found Him sitting in the temple—right in the middle of the teachers—listening and asking questions. We learn of a precious and powerful part of Jesus' growth process when the Scripture tells us those in the temple were astonished at *"His understanding and answers"* (Luke 2:47).

GROWTH INSIGHT

Strong's Concordance defines the word *"understanding"* from Luke 2:47 as literally "a mental putting together," hence, quickness of apprehension. This is comparable to the modern idiom "putting two and two together." The word here is *sunesis*, which means insight or wisdom.

Here we see Jesus, within His own personal growth process, putting two and two together. At twelve years of age, Jesus was analyzing and discerning His life according to the Scriptures. Jesus was growing in His understanding of where He had come from and who He was in the big picture.

When His parents found Him, they had a natural discussion with Him. We have to realize that even though Mary well remembered the visitation of Gabriel and the supernatural birth of Jesus, and knew fully who He was, this was how she spoke to Him:

> *So when they saw Him, they were amazed; and His mother said to Him, "Son, why have You done this to us? Look, Your father and I have sought You anxiously."...Then He went down with them and came to Nazareth, and was subject to them, but His mother kept all these things in her heart.* (Luke 2:48, 51)

Notice the key word, *"subject."* We see that, in Jesus' growth process, even as the Son of God, He remained under the care and guidance of His earthly parents.

> *And Jesus increased in wisdom and stature, and in favor with God and men.* (Luke 2:52)

Just because you're alive and enjoy life, this does not mean you will automatically experience spiritual and personal growth. As Jesus increased in wisdom and in favor with God and men, this is also God's expectation for you.

WEEK ONE

THE FEAR OF GOD

week
one

THE FEAR OF GOD

*Especially concerning the day you stood before
the LORD your God in Horeb, when the LORD said to me,
"Gather the people to Me, and I will let them hear My
words, that they may learn to fear Me all the days they live
on the earth, and that they may teach their children."*
—Deuteronomy 4:10

It's all about you.

Your heart is the most important part of your life that God desires, but He will not simply take it. You will have to give it to Him. Some people would say, "It's not about you and me. It's all about God." Of course, everything is about God. He existed before man was created and lived in an eternity of peace without the human race. But when God, in His sovereignty, chose to create man for an eternity of fellowship, friendship, and relationship, He gave much attention to earth's human race. So much that the most famous Bible verse says it all:

> *For God so loved the world that He gave His only begotten
> Son, that whoever believes in Him should not perish but
> have everlasting life.* (John 3:16)

31 DAYS OF SPIRITUAL GROWTH

Our Father God loved us so deeply He gave His only Son to save us from our sins, so that if we make the choice to receive Him as Lord and Savior and remain committed to following Him, we can live with Him forever in eternity. So then, apart from pride and arrogance, it *is* all about you. The whole theme of thirty-nine books in the Old Testament and twenty-seven in the New Testament is the dealings, corrections, and encouragements of God to His children, and His desire for His children to grow up to work as co-laborers with Him on earth.

GROWTH INSIGHT

God wants us to desire His will living in us each day.

GOD'S EVERLASTING LOVE

What then shall we say to these things? If God is for us, who can be against us? He who did not spare His own Son, but delivered Him up for us all, how shall He not with Him also freely give us all things? (Romans 8:31–32)

Therefore say to them, "Thus says the LORD of hosts: 'Return to Me,' says the LORD of hosts, 'and I will return to you,' says the LORD of hosts." (Zechariah 1:3)

God longs for us to desire to have His will, His passion, His truth, and His maturity living in us every day of our lives. Jesus came to earth to live a full life from birth to adulthood and to give us a picture of how to live our lives free from sin and disobedience. On the outside, your appearance may come across as mature and grown-up, but on the inside, the real you, your spiritual man, your emotions, your daily actions, reactions, and habits of life may be hindering God's destiny and purpose for your very existence.

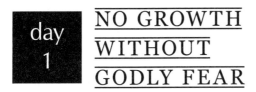

NO GROWTH WITHOUT GODLY FEAR

The fear of the LORD is the beginning of wisdom;
a good understanding have all those who do His
commandments. His praise endures forever.
—Psalm 111:10

There are two reactions that come to mind when someone mentions "the fear of God." One is a trembling-in-your-boots fear of God's power and judgment, and the other is a deep reverence that stems from honoring who God is. The fear of the Lord that leads to wisdom is this deep reverence. By "fearing God" and understanding His commandments, a person has taken the first step toward wisdom.

Unfortunately, most people today fear man and what man may say about them instead of God. God's Word teaches us not to fear man but to reverence God. *"The fear of man brings a snare, but whoever trusts in the LORD shall be safe"* (Proverbs 29:25).

When you were a little child, you needed nutritious food for energy and physical development. As a child of God, you need to be fed by His Word. You need to develop honor and godly fear. The reason there is so much concern about our children being naturally overweight and unhealthy today is that, in our culture and habits, children eat unhealthy food. The food that is best for us and our health when we are children and growing up is the kind of food we may hate to eat. How many times do children order broccoli, asparagus, and liver with their meals? Children would rather ask for ice cream, candy, and chocolate instead of fruit, a good cereal, and vegetables.

Likewise, if you are going to grow spiritually, you need to "eat" what is spiritually healthy for you: the Word of God. When you read the Word, it becomes your spiritual diet. When you "digest it"—meditate on what you have read and apply it to your life—the Bible says, *"It will be health to your flesh, and strength to your bones"* (Proverbs 3:8).

> **GROWTH INSIGHT**
>
> The Word of God is your spiritual diet.

The majority of Christians would never consider the importance of the fear of God, mainly because it is not spoken of as a positive thing. We like to hear sermons about a loving God who wants to bless us. Yet, God's Word gives us insight: *"Teach me Your way, O LORD; I will walk in Your truth; unite my heart to fear Your name"* (Psalm 86:11).

NO GROWTH LIVING IN YOUR OWN WISDOM

I n the same way that children are born with natural immaturity, when you are born again, you are spiritually immature. One aspect of this immaturity is taught to us clearly in
the Word of God. *"Do not be wise in your own eyes; fear the LORD
and depart from evil. It will be health to your flesh, and strength
to your bones"* (Proverbs 3:7–8). To be wise in your own eyes
means that you make day-to-day decisions and choices without
ever asking the Lord for wisdom and guidance.

AVOID WORLDLY WISDOM

*Let no one deceive himself. If anyone among you seems to be
wise in this age, let him become a fool that he may become
wise. For the wisdom of this world is foolishness with God.
For it is written, "He catches the wise in their own craftiness."* (1 Corinthians 3:18–19)

If your personal wisdom takes the place of godly fear, then
you are going to live in deceptive craftiness.

"Craftiness" means versatile cleverness, sophisticated
cunning, unscrupulous conduct, evil treachery, deceptive

scheming, arrogant shrewdness, and sly arrogance. This word, *"craftiness,"* is used five different times in the New Testament. It refers to Satan's deceiving Eve (2 Corinthians 11:3), the Pharisees trying to trick Jesus (Luke 20:23), the deception of false teachers (Ephesians 4:14), the self-entrapment of the worldly wise (1 Corinthians 3:19), and using deceit when presenting the gospel (2 Corinthians 4:2).

> **GROWTH INSIGHT**
>
> Godly fear leads to true wisdom.

You will always maintain a spiritual childishness if your own crafty wisdom takes the place of godly fear in your life.

LACK OF
GODLY FEAR
FEEDS DECEPTION
AND FAILURE

*The fear of the LORD is the beginning of knowledge, but
fools despise wisdom and instruction.*
—Proverbs 1:7

The kind of knowledge that comes from the fear of the
Lord is not scientific, social, or political. It is the knowledge of a very personal relationship with God. *"The secret
of the LORD is with those who fear Him, and He will show them
His covenant"* (Psalm 25:14). God reveals His secret counsel
in close friendships, as He did with Abraham, who feared the
Lord (see Genesis 18:17–19; James 2:23), and as He did with
the apostles. (See John 15:15.)

The Bible tells us a story of how a lack of godly fear brought
death to two well-meaning people. But God used this absence
of fear in the early church to create godly fear and bring growth
and knowledge of who He is. At the end of Acts, chapter two,
time had passed since the day of Pentecost. The followers of
Jesus had been empowered by the presence of God and the

actual birthing of the church. Multitudes had been saved, many people had been healed, and lives had been changed for the good. No one was lacking anything. Everyone was in a sharing mood. Many with possessions sold them and brought the proceeds to the apostles for distribution to the needy. Acts 4:36–37 says, *"And Joses, who was also named Barnabas by the apostles (which is translated Son of Encouragement), a Levite of the country of Cyprus, having land, sold it, and brought the money and laid it at the apostles' feet."* Cyprus was an island abundantly blessed with natural resources. It was famous for its flowers and fruits. Wine and oil were produced there in abundance. A variety of precious stones were also found in Cyprus, but its chief source of wealth was in its mines and forests. It had extensive silver, copper, and iron mines. Cyprus was a country overflowing in natural wealth. Back then, if you owned land on Cyprus, you were probably wealthy.

> **GROWTH INSIGHT**
>
> What matters in giving is the attitude of our hearts.

Picture this event: a wealthy Levite named Barnabas from another land brought the total amount of money he received from the sale of his property, which was probably a very large sum, and placed it at the apostles' disposal. *"But a certain man named Ananias, with Sapphira his wife, sold a possession"* (Acts 5:1). Notice the first word in this sentence, *"But."* By the use of this word, it is obvious that what has just happened in the fourth chapter of Acts with Barnabas is tied to the record of Ananias and Sapphira in the fifth chapter of Acts.

WHAT IS HAPPENING?

A newcomer who was very wealthy joined the church and brought a very large offering consisting of the sale price of his land. Barnabas' offering caused Ananias and Sapphira to react by selling something they owned.

> *And he kept back part of the proceeds, his wife also being aware of it, and brought a certain part and laid it at the apostles' feet. But Peter* [The supernatural gift of knowledge was working here.] *said, "Ananias, why has Satan filled your heart to lie to the Holy Spirit and keep back part of the price of the land for yourself? While it remained, was it not your own? And after it was sold, was it not in your own control? Why have you conceived this thing in your heart? You have not lied to men but to God."* (Acts 5:2–4)

It's possible that the people had conversed among themselves about how Barnabas' great gift would help so many people. It was probably the "talk of the town." So Ananias and Sapphira may have said to themselves, "We will sell our prized possession of land, but this is just too much to give away. We cannot give it all, but we will appear to be giving it all." Together they agreed to withhold some of the profit for themselves.

> **GROWTH INSIGHT**
>
> Lying and deception was their sin because they lacked the fear of God.

It was not wrong to keep some of the money from the sale, but they pretended they had given their entire profit. Their deception was the issue, not the money. They wanted the praises of men more than they valued truth and integrity. If you and I desire the praise of men, we will fear man. If you and I fear man, we will serve him, because we serve what we fear. Ananias and Sapphira were more concerned with earthly wealth and reputation than what God would think of their deception. If they had had a fear of God, they never would have lied in His presence.

Then Ananias, hearing these words, fell down and breathed his last. So great fear came upon all those who heard these things. And the young men arose and wrapped him up, carried him out, and buried him. Now it was about three hours later when his wife came in, not knowing what had happened. And Peter answered her, "Tell me whether you sold the land for so much?" She said, "Yes, for so much." Then Peter said to her, "How is it that you have agreed together to test the Spirit of the Lord? Look, the feet of those who have buried your husband are at the door, and they will carry you out." Then immediately she fell down at his feet and breathed her last. And the young men came in and found her dead, and carrying her out, buried her by her husband.

(Acts 5:5–10)

The result was,

Great fear came upon all the church and upon all who heard these things. (Acts 5:11)

You may still do some good things, even if you lack godly fear. However, a lack of godly fear will soon lead to self-deception, and it will eventually destroy you.

CONTINUED IMMATURITY RESISTS THE FEAR OF GOD

day 4

The church had been enjoying the presence of the Lord and all His benefits. When the people were filled with the Holy Spirit in Acts 2, others accused them of acting like drunken men because of the powerful influence of the Holy Spirit in their lives. But maybe with the passing of time, people became too familiar with the presence of God.

INSIGHT:

Maybe some had heard how approachable Jesus had been and decided now that their relationship with the Holy Spirit would become similar. Even though the Father, Son, and Spirit are one, there is a difference between them. Even Jesus said men could speak against Him and it would be forgiven, but not if they spoke against the Holy Spirit.

IMPORTANT:

Before Jesus came to earth, the people had been afraid or scared of God without having a godly fear of Him. When Jesus came, He taught people to consider God as their Father, and the people may have started taking Him for granted. Now in Acts 5, a balance had to be restored. The church woke up to the holiness of God when Ananias and Sapphira fell dead at Peter's feet. About this time, some may have wondered, *Maybe we should rethink some things.* Others may have thought, *That could easily have been me.* Still others, I believe, had their concept of God jolted or shaken. *I guess I don't know God as well as I thought I did. I'm surprised at God's swift and severe judgment.* The Bible teaches us, *"He who dwells in the secret place of the Most High shall abide under the shadow of the Almighty"* (Psalm 91:1). Only when we fear God will we find this secret refuge.

> **GROWTH INSIGHT**
>
> **A place of secret refuge can be found in God.**

> *The secret of the LORD is with those who fear Him, and He will show them His covenant.*　　　　　(Psalm 25:14)

CHILDISH CARELESSNESS

Childish carelessness ignores godly fear. Ananias and Sapphira were a part of the crowd that was excited about the revival over the previous few years and the unusual signs and wonders, but because they lacked a *fear* of God, they had no restraint from carelessness.

> *Come, you children, listen to me; I will teach you the fear of the LORD. Who is the man who desires life, and loves many days, that he may see good?…Depart from evil and do good; seek peace and pursue it.*　　　　　(Psalm 34:11–12, 14)

day 5 — FEAR OF THE LORD ENDURES

f Lucifer had possessed the fear of God, he never would
have fallen from heaven.

> *How you are fallen from heaven, O Lucifer, son of the morn-*
> *ing! How you are cut down to the ground, you who weakened*
> *the nations! For you have said in your heart: "I will ascend*
> *into heaven, I will exalt my throne above the stars of God;*
> *I will also sit on the mount of the congregation on the far-*
> *thest sides of the north; I will ascend above the heights of the*
> *clouds, I will be like the Most High."*   (Isaiah 14:12–14)
>
> *The fear of the LORD is clean, enduring forever.*
>   (Psalm 19:9)

Lucifer was the anointed cherub on the holy mountain of
God and walked in the presence of the Lord, but he was the
first to reveal a lack of the fear of God. (See Ezekiel 28:14–
15.) Adam and Eve loved and benefited from God's goodness.
They lived in a perfect environment, and they never would
have fallen if they had possessed the fear of God. *"In mercy and*
*truth atonement is provided for iniquity; and by the **fear** of the LORD*
one departs from evil" (Proverbs 16:6, emphasis added).

In Jim Bakker's book, entitled *I Was Wrong,* he shared with someone who visited him in prison that the "heat" of the prison had caused him to have a complete change of heart. He said that he had experienced Jesus as Master for the first time in his life. He said to his visitor, "This prison is not God's judgment on my life, but His mercy. I believe if I had continued on the path that I was on I would have ended up in hell." Jim further explained, "I always loved Jesus, yet He was not my Lord, and there are millions like me." Jim's love for Jesus was immature because he lacked the fear of God. Jim said, "If I get out of prison and go back to the way I was, I will be judged."

THE BLESSINGS OF FEARING GOD

Let us hear the conclusion of the whole matter: Fear God and keep His commandments, for this is man's all. For God will bring every work into judgment, including every secret thing, whether good or evil.

(Ecclesiastes 12:13–14)

The fear of God gives Him the place of glory, honor, reverence, thanksgiving, and praise, and the preeminence, He desires. It is what God deserves, not what we think He deserves, that matters.

Godly Fear Assures Us That His Goodness Abounds

Oh, how great is Your goodness, which You have laid up for those who fear You, which You have prepared for those who trust in You in the presence of the sons of men!

(Psalm 31:19)

Godly Fear Promises Angelic Protection

The angel of the LORD encamps all around those who fear Him, and delivers them. (Psalm 34:7)

Godly Fear Secures God's Continual Attention

Behold, the eye of the LORD is on those who fear Him, on those who hope in His mercy. (Psalm 33:18)

Godly Fear Supplies His Provision

Oh, fear the LORD, you His saints! There is no want to those who fear Him. (Psalm 34:9)

Godly Fear Contains Great Mercy

For as the heavens are high above the earth, so great is His mercy toward those who fear Him. (Psalm 103:11)

Godly Fear Promises Protection

You who fear the LORD, trust in the LORD; He is their help and their shield. (Psalm 115:11)

Godly Fear Fulfills Our Desires and Delivers Us from Harm

He will fulfill the desire of those who fear Him; He also will hear their cry and save them. (Psalm 145:19)

Godly Fear Provides Wisdom, Understanding, and Time Management

The fear of the LORD is the beginning of wisdom, and the knowledge of the Holy One is understanding. For by me your days will be multiplied, and years of life will be added to you. (Proverbs 9:10–11)

31 DAYS OF SPIRITUAL GROWTH

Godly Fear Provides Peace of Mind

Better is a little with the fear of the Lord, than great treasure with trouble. (Proverbs 15:16)

Godly Fear Is Our Confidence and Protection in the Face of Death

In the fear of the LORD there is strong confidence, and His children will have a place of refuge. The fear of the LORD is a fountain of life, to turn one away from the snares of death. (Proverbs 14:26–27)

Godly Fear Results in Complete Satisfaction

The fear of the LORD leads to life, and he who has it will abide in satisfaction; He will not be visited with evil.
(Proverbs 19:23)

Godly Fear with Humility Brings Great Gain

By humility and the fear of the Lord are riches and honor and life. (Proverbs 22:4)

Godly Fear Builds a Secure Home

And so it was, because the midwives feared God, that He provided households for them. (Exodus 1:21)

Godly Fear Causes Joyful, Satisfying Labor and a Fruitful Life

Blessed is every one who fears the LORD, who walks in His ways. When you eat the labor of your hands, you shall be happy, and it shall be well with you. Your wife shall be like

*a fruitful vine in the very heart of your house, your chil-
dren like olive plants all around your table. Behold, thus
shall the man be blessed who fears the LORD.*

(Psalm 128:1–4)

GODLY FEAR PRODUCES EXCELLENT LEADERSHIP

*Moreover you shall select from all the people able men, such
as fear God, men of truth, hating covetousness; and place
such over them to be rulers of thousands, rulers of hundreds,
rulers of fifties, and rulers of tens.* (Exodus 18:21)

*The God of Israel said, the Rock of Israel spoke to me:
"He who rules over men must be just, ruling in the fear of
God."* (2 Samuel 23:3)

If you will pray and ask the Lord Jesus by His Holy Spirit
to develop godly fear in your life, you will be strong and endure every hit and disappointment that comes against you.

GROWTH INSIGHT

Godly fear is
the key to a
blessed life.

<table>
<tr>
<td>day
6</td>
<td>

GODLY FEAR
RECEIVED IS
YOUR FIRST MARK
OF MATURITY

</td>
</tr>
</table>

How well do you get along with other people? The fear of God in your life will lead you to ask important, everyday, commonsense questions such as: How well do I get along with other people? Life involves us with people. It is unscriptural to be a lone person and especially a lone Christian. At times it seems easier to ignore involvement with others, but by living this way, we never face deep-rooted problems and hurts, and we continue the same old routines.

We need one another for balance and growth; growing up with maturity is impossible without each other. (See John 17:11, 21, 23.) A growing fear of God in us will help us to adjust socially with our bosses, others in authority, other Christians, and especially our families. These are the real heart issues of life. (See Matthew 22:36–40.) Real growth and maturity in life is nurtured in relationship.

GODLY FEAR DEVELOPS MARKS OF MATURITY

Do you have contentment? Contentment is one of God's most precious treasures. *"Now godliness with contentment is great gain"* (1 Timothy 6:6). The apostle Paul said, *"Not that I speak in regard to need, for I have learned in whatever state I am, to be content"* (Philippians 4:11). Paul did not have a beautiful home, the comfort of an understanding wife, fancy clothes, or any of the luxuries of life. Instead Paul had suffered the loss of all things, including his past positions and titles and the honor of man. (See Philippians 3:7–10.) Many Christians who are trying to grow up keep drinking from the polluted streams of earth in an attempt to satisfy their thirsty souls. But the apostle Paul found the secret to contentment and joy with very little of this world's pleasures. Paul's joy came from the source that matured him. He connected with Christ in a personal way and continued to drink deeply of His life.

> **GROWTH INSIGHT**
>
> The pleasures of the world don't give true peace and joy.

You will show me the path of life; in Your presence is fullness of joy; at Your right hand are pleasures forevermore.

(Psalm 16:11)

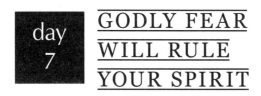

GODLY FEAR WILL RULE YOUR SPIRIT

He who is slow to anger is better than
the mighty, and he who rules his spirit
than he who takes a city.
—Proverbs 16:32

A Christian is not growing up very fast and is far from being mature when he is ruled and dominated by his emotions, has outbursts of wrath, and has not learned to handle hurt feelings. Ruling our spirits means disciplining our feelings and immature habits. The ability to say no comes because we allow God's grace to develop our lives through personal training in cooperation with Holy Spirit disciplines. It is very important to discipline our emotions, because out of our emotions spring many of life's actions and decisions. *"Keep your heart with all diligence, for out of it spring the issues of life"* (Proverbs 4:23).

CHANGE YOUR BELIEF SYSTEM

For we know Him who said, "Vengeance is Mine, I will
repay," says the Lord. And again, "The LORD will judge

His people." It is a fearful thing to fall into the hands of the living God. (Hebrews 10:30–31)

Until the fear of God becomes a part of your belief system, you can never grow up. You will never change your life until you change your belief system. Embracing the fear of God in your life will move you from failure to success in every aspect of life.

A wise man will hear and increase learning, and a man of understanding will attain wise counsel. (Proverbs 1:5)

GROWTH INSIGHT

Until the fear of God becomes part of your belief system, you can never grow up.

WHAT DOES IT MEAN TO GROW UP?

week
two

WHAT DOES IT MEAN
TO GROW UP?

*I said, "O my God, do not take me away
in the midst of my days; Your years are
throughout all generations."*
—Psalm 102:24

Growing up in the natural may look good in the mirror, but it is also a time of constant frustration, mistakes, bad choices, and discord in your life. You are also, for the first time, waking up in your spirit and soul. Though you may look like an adult on the outside, on the inside you may still whine and act like an immature child.

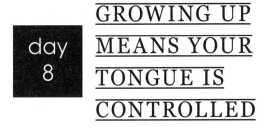

day 8

GROWING UP MEANS YOUR TONGUE IS CONTROLLED

The Word says that the man who has control over his tongue is a perfect man. *"For we all stumble in many things. If anyone does not stumble in word, he is a perfect man, able also to bridle the whole body"* (James 3:2).

Growing up in spirit and soul is always a heart issue.

> *A good* [mature] *man out of the good treasure of his heart brings forth good; and an evil man out of the evil treasure of his heart brings forth evil. For out of the abundance of the heart his mouth speaks.* (Luke 6:45)

We have to learn that God desires to mature us, not just deliver us from difficult situations we have brought upon ourselves.

> *And the LORD restored Job's losses when he prayed for his friends. Indeed the LORD gave Job twice as much as he had before.* (Job 42:10)

Does Your Tongue Keep Secrets?

"A talebearer reveals secrets, but he who is of a faithful spirit conceals a matter" (Proverbs 11:13). How mature are you? Have you grown enough in your spirit man to resist the temptation to reveal the confidential matters of others? God corrected Ham in a very strong way for telling his brothers of his father Noah's nakedness instead of honoring him and covering him, as his brothers Shem and Japheth did. (See Genesis 9:20–27.)

GROWTH INSIGHT

Control over the tongue is one of the hardest things to master, but it is essential to maturity.

Is Your Tongue Full of Negative Confessions?

In the Bible, the story of the spies sent into the Promised Land shows how devastating and discouraging negative confessions can be. The ten spies with the bad report discouraged the whole congregation of Israel, leading them to murmur and harden themselves against the prosperity and promises of God. (See Numbers 13:26–14:10; 32:9).

And you complained in your tents, and said, "Because the LORD hates us, He has brought us out of the land of Egypt to deliver us into the hand of the Amorites, to destroy us."

(Deuteronomy 1:27)

IS YOUR TONGUE HOOKED TO FLATTERY?

Flattery can be a major obstacle to your growth process. Satan is a talker, a flatterer. He uses flattery as bait. It is so easy for people to take the bait of flattery and get hooked before they realize it. A nice and honest word of encouragement is good and right; however, flattery is different; its motive is deceitful. It is always looking for a payoff (the hook). *"A lying tongue hates those who are crushed by it, and a flattering mouth works ruin"* (Proverbs 26:28). The fruit of flattery is self-deception, an immature heart hooked by smooth words.

DOES YOUR TONGUE SAY JUST ANYTHING?

"You are snared by the words of your mouth; you are taken by the words of your mouth" (Proverbs 6:2). The flesh can lead our mouths to sin by making promises, vows, and commitments we later regret or are unable to keep. God wants to mature us by helping us develop a sense of caution in regard to what we say.

DOES YOUR TONGUE UNDERSTAND THE CHILDISHNESS OF DISCORD?

The Word says that there are six main things the Lord hates, two of which are *"a false witness who speaks lies, and one who sows discord among brethren"* (Proverbs 6:19). Your enemy, Satan, has a plan for your life that includes stunting your maturity and your joining him in hell. His greatest weapon against you comes from his mouth:

Then I heard a loud voice saying in heaven, "Now salvation, and strength, and the kingdom of our God, and the power of His Christ have come, for the accuser of our brethren, who accused them before our God day and night, has been cast down." (Revelation 12:10)

The power of this weapon does not come from his ability to convince God, for God knows the truth and Christ died for all the things the enemy uses to accuse us. The power lies in his ability to convince us of our condemnation by his accusations and to encourage us to take up his weapon against others. When we take up the role of accuser or judge against others it always backfires.

Judge not, that you be not judged. For with what judgment you judge, you will be judged; and with the measure you use, it will be measured back to you.

(Matthew 7:1–2)

GROWING UP MEANS YOUR PRIDE IS CONQUERED

There are two kinds of spiritual warfare. The first is the kind that comes to you simply because you are a confessing Christian made in the image of God. It is called "life's warfare." The second kind of warfare is called "unnecessary warfare." A person creates this kind for himself through continued wrong choices and pride. Often Satan is not our greatest enemy—we are!

Pride is the number one problem of self, and it is at the root of most of our difficulties and torments. It is impossible to grow up until pride has been buried in your life—and it doesn't like to stay buried! Pride makes us pretend to be something we are not. It demands recognition. When a proud person goes unnoticed, he becomes angry and easily offended. This seed, if cultivated, bears the fruit of hatred, depression, self-pity, bitterness, and separation from God. In contrast, godly humility produces the fruit of spiritual health and a mature growth process. *"Let not the foot of pride come against me, and let not the hand of the wicked drive me away"* (Psalm 36:11). Pride also gives a false sense of security that quickly gives way, with disastrous results.

> *Pride goes before destruction, and a haughty spirit before a fall.* (Proverbs 16:18)

"A man's pride will bring him low, but the humble in spirit will retain honor" (Proverbs 29:23). Godly maturity trusts that the Lord will exalt and make room for you.

GROWTH INSIGHT

Pride is the number one problem of self.

GROWING UP MEANS PATIENCE IS A FOUNDATION

day 10

Patience is the quality of maturity that pauses to consider all the choices carefully and does not make quick judgments or jump to hasty conclusions. It waits on the Lord even when He seems to be silent. The person who makes quick decisions all the time is one who lives in turmoil brought on by himself.

> *He who answers a matter before he hears it, it is folly and shame to him.* (Proverbs 18:13)

Patience is rare even among those who consider themselves to be mature and growing Christians. It may be gained by passing through many hard times. *"And not only that, but we also glory in tribulations, knowing that tribulation produces perseverance"* (Romans 5:3). A growing and mature person is recognized by the fruit of patience in his life. The Bible has much to say about being rooted, grounded, established, and solid. Many believers live an "up and down" life because they are controlled by their mood swings rather than waiting on God to fulfill His truth. Christians who are growing up and moving forward are not controlled by their feelings or circumstances, but by faith and trust in God. Paul said to the Corinthian Christians, *"For we walk by faith, not by sight"* (2 Corinthians 5:7). It is this faith, this patience, rather than reacting to the immediate situation, that leads to godly wisdom and maturity.

> ### GROWTH INSIGHT
>
> Patience is gained by going through hard times.

day 11

GROWING UP MEANS YOU ARE A SERVANT

A ccording to Jesus, greatness in the kingdom of God is determined by humility, or by how much of a servant's heart has been developed in our lives.

Then He [Jesus] came to Capernaum. And when He was in the house He asked them, "What was it you disputed among yourselves on the road?" But they kept silent, for on the road they had disputed among themselves who would be the greatest. And He sat down, called the twelve, and said to them, "If anyone desires to be first, he shall be last of all and servant of all." (Mark 9:33–35)

A SERVANT'S HEART

A servant is:

- Someone who is committed to meeting the needs of others, just the opposite of someone who is self-centered. (See Philippians 2:29–21.)

- Not demanding—no one poor in spirit has a demanding attitude. (See Matthew 5:3.)

- Not independent—a servant puts up with inconvenience so that the greater good may be accomplished. He endures because he sees the bigger picture. (See 1 Corinthians 9:19.)

- One who will do more than asked to do—not requiring a "thank you" or recognition (See Luke 17:7–10.)

GROWTH INSIGHT

The true servant fulfills the law of love, which is total unselfishness.

GOD KNOWS WHERE YOU ARE AND HE'S GOT YOUR NUMBER

day 12

Dear friends, by this time you may be wondering, *Is it really necessary to grow up? Does God even care that much about my life?* You need to be encouraged that God is *for* you and He is *always* there.

The following message is a tremendous story of encouragement that illustrates this point. This true account is told by minister Ken Grub:

> Do you believe that God not only loves you, but knows where you are and what you're doing every minute of the day? I certainly do after an amazing experience I had several years ago. On this particular day I was driving on I-75 near Dayton, Ohio, with my wife and children. We turned off the highway for a rest and refreshment stop. My wife, Barbara, and the children went into the restaurant. I suddenly felt the need to stretch my legs, so I waved them ahead, saying I'd join them later. I bought a soft drink and as I

61

walked toward a Dairy Queen, feelings of self-pity en-shrouded my mind. I loved the Lord and my ministry, but I felt drained, burdened. My emotional cup was empty. Suddenly the impatient ringing of a telephone nearby jarred me out of my heaviness. It was coming from a phone booth at a service station on the corner. I thought, *Isn't anyone going to answer the phone?* Noise from the traffic rushing through the busy intersection must have drowned out the sound, because the service station attendant continued looking after his customers, oblivious to the continued ringing.

"Why doesn't someone answer that phone?" I muttered. I began reasoning, *It may be important. What if it's an emergency?* Curiosity overcame my indifference, so I stepped inside the booth and picked up the phone. "Hello," I said casually and took a big sip of my drink. The operator said, "Long distance call for Ken Grub." My eyes widened, and I almost choked on a chunk of ice. Swallowing hard, I said, "You're crazy!" Then, realizing I shouldn't speak to an operator like that, I added, "This can't be! I was walking down the road, not bothering anyone, and the phone was ringing...."

"Is Ken Grub there?" the operator interrupted. "I have a long distance call for him." It took a moment to gain control of my babbling, but I finally replied, "Yes, he is here." Searching for a possible explanation, I wondered if I could possibly be on *Candid Camera*. Still shaken and perplexed, I asked, "How in the world did you reach me here? I was just walking down the road, the phone started ringing, and I just answered it on chance. You can't mean me!"

"Well," the operator asked, "is Mr. Grub there or isn't he?"

"Yes, I am Ken Grub," I said, finally convinced by the tone of her voice that the call was real. Then I heard another voice say, "Yes, that's him, operator. That's Ken Grub." I listened, dumbfounded, to a strange voice identifying herself. "I'm from Harrisburg, Pennsylvania. You don't know me, Mr. Grub, but I'm desperate. Please help me."

"What can I do for you?"

She began weeping. Finally she regained control and continued. "I was about to commit suicide, had just finished writing a note, when I began to pray and tell God I didn't really want to do this. Then I suddenly remembered seeing you on television and thought if I could just talk to you, you could help me. I knew that was impossible because I didn't know how to reach you. I didn't know anyone who could help me find you. Then some numbers came to my mind, and I scribbled the numbers down."

At this point she began weeping again, and I prayed silently for wisdom to help her. She continued, "I looked at the numbers and thought, 'Wouldn't it be wonderful if I had a miracle from God, and He has given me Ken's phone number?' I decided to try calling it. I can't believe I'm talking to you....Are you in your office in California?"

"My office is in Yakima, Washington. How can I help you?"

A little surprised, she asked, "Don't you know?"

I responded, "You made the call."

She explained, "But I don't even know what area I'm calling. I just dialed the number that I had on this paper...."

"Ma'am, you won't believe this, but I'm in a phone booth in Dayton, Ohio."

"Really?" she answered. "Well, what are you doing there?"

I kidded her gently, "Well, I'm answering the phone. It was ringing as I walked by, so I answered it."

Knowing the encounter could only have been arranged by God, I began to counsel the woman. As she told me of her despair and frustration, the presence of the Holy Spirit flooded the phone booth, giving me words of wisdom beyond my ability. In a matter of minutes, she prayed the sinner's prayer and met the One who could lead her out of her situation into a new life.

I walked away from that telephone booth with an electrifying sense of our heavenly Father's concern for each of His children. What were the astronomical odds of this happening? With all the millions of phones and innumerable combinations of numbers, only an all-knowing God could have caused that woman to call that number in that phone booth at that moment in time.

Forgetting my drink and nearly bursting with exhilaration, I headed back to my family, wondering if they could believe my story. *Maybe I'd better not tell this,*

I thought, but I couldn't contain it. "Barb, you won't believe this! God knows where I am!"

God also knows where you are. Place yourself in His hands, concentrate on knowing His will for your life, and He will never forsake you.

GROWTH INSIGHT

God is watching you at every moment, ready to step in with a miracle when you need it most.

What a great story to encourage you in your growing up process. How wonderful it is to know that God is lovingly watching you every moment. He wants you to always desire growth and maturity in your life. Not only that, He is always on standby to help you with a miracle in your growth process.

How precious also are Your thoughts to me, O God! How great is the sum of them! If I should count them, they would be more in number than the sand; when I awake, I am still with You. (Psalm 139:17–18)

day 13

GROWING UP MEANS RESPECTING AUTHORITY

T he degree to which we are submitted to the Lord is revealed by how we react to those people whom God places in positions of authority over us. God works and speaks primarily through men and women. He honors offices of leadership. On a regular basis, God is speaking to us through human agents, such as husbands, wives, teachers, pastors, and law officers. So when these agents are being ignored, God is being ignored. (See Romans 13:1–7.)

A good example of this is the story of Eli the high priest in 1 Samuel 1–3. Even though Eli was a priest, he was not living according to the laws of God. In this backslidden condition, he observed a woman named Hannah in the temple one day. He assumed she was drunk and rebuked her harshly. He used his position to sit in judgment of her. Hannah was not drunk, but was instead crying out to God for a son, because she was barren. When she explained the reason for her weeping, Eli replied, *"Go in peace, and the God of Israel grant your petition which you have asked of Him"* (1 Samuel 1:17). God honored the words and blessings of Eli. He honored Eli's office, though He did not necessarily honor the man. Hannah responded in faith, and she returned home and later gave birth to little Samuel. This woman is an excellent example of a mature and growing woman of God who was wise enough to discern God speaking through man. She put aside her hurts and rejections and listened to God's voice coming through a man who, though he was in a position of authority, was spiritually immature himself.

MATURITY IS ATTITUDE

We are called to submission to wives or husbands, regardless of their moods (see Ephesians 5:21), and the same is true toward law officers or employers.

> *Therefore submit yourselves to every ordinance of man for the Lord's sake, whether to the king as supreme, or to governors, as to those who are sent by him for the punishment of evildoers and for the praise of those who do good.*
>
> (1 Peter 2:13–14)

> *Servants, be submissive to your masters with all fear, not only to the good and gentle, but also to the harsh.*
>
> (1 Peter 2:18)

The person who says, "I am just not going to listen to any man. I listen only to the Lord," is not listening to the Lord either. God speaks to us today through His Word and through those in authority over us. God's Holy Spirit teaches us how to submit and listen to those whom God has placed over us.

GROWTH INSIGHT

God speaks to us through His Word and through others.

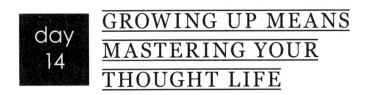

day 14   GROWING UP MEANS MASTERING YOUR THOUGHT LIFE

I t is impossible to get very far in the growth process without first controlling your thought life. Every victory or defeat in life is won or lost through the meditation of the mind. By the choice of what we meditate upon, we are feeding either the new nature or the old nature.

> *Hear, O earth! Behold, I will certainly bring calamity on this people; the fruit of their thoughts, because they have not heeded My words, nor My law, but rejected it.*
>
> (Jeremiah 6:19)

THOUGHTS BECOME ACTIONS

Discouragement is the inevitable result of meditating upon, agreeing with, and speaking what your enemy is saying about you and your situation rather than what God's Word is saying. God's attitude and thoughts are always positive toward us.

> *For I know the thoughts that I think toward you, says the LORD, thoughts of peace and not of evil, to give you a future and a hope.*
>
> (Jeremiah 29:11)

Sin is conceived in the thought life. It grows as you meditate upon it and then is birthed into action. Sin doesn't just happen. People sin (the action) because they have allowed sin (the thought) to take up residence in their minds. Wrong thoughts feed evil habits.

> *Therefore do not let sin reign in your mortal body, that you should obey it in its lusts. And do not present your members as instruments of unrighteousness to sin, but present yourselves to God as being alive from the dead, and your members as instruments of righteousness to God. For sin shall not have dominion over you, for you are not under law but under grace.* (Romans 6:12–14)

Right thinking will weaken evil habits and release your growth process to advance to the next level. There will be no consistent victory in your active life until you learn to control your thought life. You must "take every thought captive" in order to grow in maturity. (See 2 Corinthians 10:5.)

"Therefore gird up the loins of your mind, be sober, and rest your hope fully upon the grace that is to be brought to you at the revelation of Jesus Christ" (1 Peter 1:13). What does it mean to gird up the loins of the mind? In Bible days a man wore long, flowing garments. This loose clothing was cool and comfortable for everyday walking, but when he decided to go on a journey, the loose robes were cumbersome. In order to facilitate walking, a man would reach down and tightly tuck the garments under his belt, and off he would travel. This

> **GROWTH INSIGHT**
>
> Consistent victory comes when you can control your thoughts.

was called girding up the loins. Peter instructed us to do the same with our minds. When we are spiritually immature, our thoughts run unchecked. As long as we don't want to get anywhere, this will do. But if we want to make spiritual progress, we must restrain our thought life. By a choice of maturity, we have the God-given power to direct our thoughts and change our focus.

WEEK THREE

REFUSING TO GROW UP
FEEDS WEAKNESS

REFUSING TO GROW UP
FEEDS WEAKNESS

*Now there was a long war between the house of Saul
and the house of David. But David grew stronger and
stronger, and the house of Saul grew weaker and weaker.*
—2 Samuel 3:1

A person who refuses to grow up spiritually and emotionally, developing godly character and integrity,
will eventually, like King Saul, destroy himself and
miss God's destiny for his life.

> *Therefore let him who thinks he stands take heed lest he
> fall.* (1 Corinthians 10:12)

Our physical bodies need food for strength and health.
If we were to stop eating for a long period of time, we would
grow weaker and weaker until we could no longer function
normally. The same is true for spiritual and emotional growth.
If you say, "I am a Christian," and just keep living any way you
please, without any marks of growth or maturity, you will get
weaker and weaker until you find yourself in a very vulnerable
position. The Bible teaches that David got stronger, but Saul
got weaker; I don't think this meant just in military strength,
but also in attitude toward God and life.

REFUSING TO GROW UP HINDERS FINANCIAL INTEGRITY

day 15

There are 2,702 verses in the Bible relating to money. How we handle money has a direct connection to our Christian growth. I believe this is the reason Jesus mentioned this subject in two-thirds of His parable teachings. A major financial principle we glean from them is, "It is not how much money we have, but how well we manage what God gives us."

HOW WE MANAGE MONEY EXPOSES
STRENGTH OR WEAKNESS

1. Do we have a good conscience?
2. Do we have good priorities?
3. How do we use our time?
4. Do we use good judgment?
5. Are we living in faith or doubt?
6. Do we know anything about sacrifice?
7. Are we walking in obedience?
8. Are we living in discipline and self-control?
9. Are we totally committed to the Lord?

Many believers' immaturity shows up through lack of financial integrity. Too often Christian bookstores are unable to give credit to many confessing Christians because of the difficulty of collecting what is owed. Bible schools have had to change their policies because so many students have failed to pay their overdue tuition fees. It is very immature to have outstanding debts and at the same time continue to add to the financial burden by buying new and expensive items. Paul gave a command, not a suggestion or recommendation, *"Owe no one anything except to love one another, for he who loves another has fulfilled the law"* (Romans 13:8).

GROWTH INSIGHT

The way we manage money shows us where our heart is. If we serve God, we use our money to honor Him.

YOU CANNOT SERVE GOD AND RICHES

He who is faithful in what is least is faithful also in much; and he who is unjust in what is least is unjust also in much. Therefore if you have not been faithful in the unrighteous mammon, who will commit to your trust the true riches? And if you have not been faithful in what is another man's, who will give you what is your own? (Luke 16:10–12)

Jesus was saying that to be undependable in financial matters indicates that we would also be undependable in spiritual matters. Handling money, from God's perspective, is a matter of the heart. God will always test us in the natural things of life, such as our jobs, family, and money. If we pass His test in these matters, then we will qualify for the *"true riches"* of God's blessings, favor, and authority in our daily lives. How we handle the resources God has given us is very important to our heavenly Father and His destiny for us.

Three Main Reasons for Financial Bondage

Failure to tithe. It is impossible to be blessed if we do not tithe. *"Honor the Lord with your possessions, and with the firstfruits of all your increase; so your barns will be filled with plenty, and your vats will overflow with new wine"* (Proverbs 3:9–10).

We are literally stealing from God when the tithe is not paid.

> *"Will a man rob God? Yet you have robbed Me! But you say, 'In what way have we robbed You?' In tithes and offerings. You are cursed with a curse, for you have robbed Me, even this whole nation. Bring all the tithes into the storehouse, that there may be food in My house, and try Me now in this," says the Lord of hosts, "If I will not open for you the windows of heaven and pour out for you such blessing that there will not be room enough to receive it."*
>
> (Malachi 3:8–10)

The key here is that when we honor the Lord with the first and very best of our income, He says, *"'I will rebuke the devourer for your sakes, so that he will not destroy the fruit of your ground, nor shall the vine fail to bear fruit for you in the field'"* (Malachi 3:11). Devourers are anything that steals away our finances. In Malachi, the devourer came in the form of a blight that diminished all their crops. There are devourers today that constantly drain our resources, such as hospital bills, car repairs, and many other things.

Tithing is not only an ordinance of the law; it also preceded the age of the law. Abraham paid tithes to Melchizedek. (See Genesis 14:18–20.) In the New Testament, Jesus preached tithing as well. In Matthew 23:23, the people were tithing but neglecting the more important matters of the law, such as mercy, justice, and the love of God. Concerning tithing, Jesus declared, *"These you ought to have done, without leaving the others undone."* He was saying that tithing is an obligation and that we should continue to do it, while not forgetting the other important matters of the law of life.

> **GROWTH INSIGHT**
>
> We should give in faith, trusting God to provide.

But this I say: He who sows sparingly will also reap sparingly, and he who sows bountifully will also reap bountifully. So let each one give as he purposes in his heart, not grudgingly or of necessity; for God loves a cheerful giver.

(2 Corinthians 9:6–7)

The attitude with which we give is also important to God. Growing up in this area of life requires that we ask God our Father to develop in us a desire to give cheerfully and not out of compulsion. We should always give in faith, knowing that God is always our provider.

Mismanagement of money. We must ask ourselves the question, "Why is it that some people who have very little money are able to consistently make ends meet, while many people have much more who are always behind and in debt?"

It is very clear that mismanagement and poor judgment are the problem. We are called to be good stewards of what God provides for us.

A Few Examples of Money Mismanagement

Credit Cards: Quick, easy money soon becomes a trap. We tend to be out of control with money that is too easily available.

Overspending: Unnecessary purchases. We should bypass buying what we do not need and cannot afford.

Bad Timing: Paying excessively for items that could have been purchased for less if we had waited for the right timing. Impatience and uncontrolled desires reflect immaturity. It is better to do some research for the best bargains.

Lack of Discipline and Character. *"Whatever my eyes desired I did not keep from them. I did not withhold my heart from any pleasure, for my heart rejoiced in all my labor; and this was my reward from all my labor"* (Ecclesiastes 2:10). Solomon lacked self-control. Everything he looked at with his eyes, he went after. The whole book of Ecclesiastes is written from the perspective of a bitter old man reflecting back on his own foolishness and immaturity. Solomon tried everything under the sun in an effort to find satisfaction and happiness, but found emptiness instead.

Jesus taught this in the parable of the sower:

And when a great multitude had gathered, and they had come to Him from every city, He spoke by a parable: "A sower went out to sow his seed. And as he sowed, some fell by the wayside; and it was trampled down, and the birds of the air devoured it. Some fell on rock; and as soon as it sprang up, it withered

79

away because it lacked moisture. And some fell among thorns, and the thorns sprang up with it and choked it. But others fell on good ground, sprang up, and yielded a crop a hundred-fold." When He had said these things He cried, "He who has ears to hear, let him hear!" (Luke 8:4–8)

THE PARABLE OF THE SOWER EXPLAINED

Now the parable is this: The seed is the word of God. Those by the wayside are the ones who hear; then the devil comes and takes away the word out of their hearts, lest they should believe and be saved. But the ones on the rock are those who, when they hear, receive the word with joy; and these have no root, who believe for a while and in time of temptation fall away. Now the ones that fell among thorns are those who, when they have heard, go out and are choked with cares, riches, and pleasures of life, and bring no fruit to maturity. But the ones that fell on the good ground are those who, having heard the word with a noble and good heart, keep it and bear fruit with patience. (Luke 8:11–15)

The Lord was warning us that the cares, riches, and pleasures of this world choke out the life of the kingdom.

GROWTH INSIGHT

If you want to be poor—hoard.

If you want to be needy—grasp.

But if you want abundance—scatter.

GROWING UP MEANS LEARNING TO STOP SAYING, "IT'S NOT FAIR!"

day 16

When the complaint "It's not fair!" keeps coming out of our hearts and mouths, it clearly reveals something about our character. It shows us that we have not yet learned God's ways and that we are living in unbelief, not faith. We must come to understand deep in our hearts that we do not *deserve* anything.

> *Blessed are the poor in spirit, for theirs is the kingdom of heaven.* (Matthew 5:3)

In the original Greek, *"poor"* refers to "a clinging beggar who receives every tiny crumb with extreme gratitude." This heart attitude is just the opposite of the person who whines, "It's not fair!" and demands his share. Jesus never demanded His share or equal rights, so that should clearly be our example. It is far more common for those who are immature to experience problems with pride than with self-esteem.

81

Yet you say, "The way of the Lord is not fair." Hear now, O house of Israel, is it not My way which is fair, and your ways which are not fair? (Ezekiel 18:25)

GROWTH INSIGHT

Guilt can't change your past
any more than worry can
change your future.
—Pastor Lonnie Curl

Then He came to the disciples and found them asleep, and said to Peter, "What? Could you not watch with Me one hour? Watch and pray, lest you enter into temptation. The spirit indeed is willing, but the flesh is weak."

(Matthew 26:40–41)

GROWING UP OPENS YOUR LIFE TO FAVOR AND HOPE

Now faith is the substance of things hoped for,
the evidence of things not seen.
—Hebrews 11:1

Faith is the established conviction concerning things unseen and the settled expectation of a future reward. The Greek word translated *"substance"* literally means "a standing under," and was used in the technical sense of "title deed." The root idea is that of standing under the claim to the property to support its validity. So faith is the title deed of things hoped for. The reason that Bible faith is such a struggle for growing Christians to understand is that faith is powerless without hope. God's hope working in you sees the unseen things, which then energizes God's faith in you to bring it to pass.

As you make a decision to grow up and move on in your relationship with God, unexpected hurts will attack your life and challenge your hope in your heavenly Father. Don't be discouraged; this is just the attack of the enemy and means you are on the right track.

Discouragement Is the Enemy of Hope

My own story of the power of hope begins on April 16, 1984. My wonderful wife, Susan, our oldest son, Todd, and I had just moved to an island resort community in South Carolina where we were to become the senior pastors of a small, brand-new church. Susan was pregnant with our second son, Chad. Late that evening, at about 10:00 p.m., Susan said to me, "My water has broken. I need to go to the hospital immediately." After arriving at the hospital, Susan and I spent the next several hours together as her labor pains increased. Just before 5:00 a.m. on April 17, Susan was moved to the delivery room. I was so happy to be with her in the delivery room because I had gone through all the Lamaze classes with her just a few weeks before.

> **GROWTH INSIGHT**
>
> Hope is the confirmation that encourages you to know that you can have what you see by your spirit!

As she lay on the delivery table, we were told that her personal doctor was not available and so a substitute doctor was on his way. *This* doctor called to inform the hospital that he would probably not arrive in time, so immediately the head nurse called up an emergency room doctor to deliver this long-anticipated baby. (We found out later most emergency doctors have not had the opportunity to deliver many babies, even though, by virtue of their education, they do have some training and experience to do so.)

While Susan was lying on the table, several feet up from a hard tile floor, the emergency room doctor was talking and trying to get settled quickly for the delivery. I was at the head of the delivery table, leaning over Susan's head with a wet cloth, trying to reassure her that everything was going to be okay. The doctor had her back turned to my wife (which was certainly a medical error), and Susan had, without warning, pushed hard. She did not realize the doctor had not positioned herself properly. Susan experienced what is called a "precipitous birth."

Little Chad came out of the birth canal quickly, with no net and no one to catch him. He landed head first on a very hard tile floor. I did not see this happen, and the next thing I knew, the presiding delivery doctor had picked Chad up and handed him to a nurse standing nearby. I happened

> **GROWTH INSIGHT**
>
> God's hope does not come and go, but will live with you.

to look up and see her holding the little guy, and she said, "You've got a little boy." Not knowing what happened I said, "Is he okay?" She replied, "He fell on the floor, but he seems to be okay." Little Chad was making noises somewhat typical of a newborn baby, and it wasn't long before the procedures of cleaning Chad and Susan began. The baby was taken to a nursery, and Susan was taken to a private room.

And now abide faith, hope, love, these three; but the greatest of these is love. (1 Corinthians 13:13)

I wanted to make sure Susan was okay because she was so exhausted after being up all night and giving birth. She needed to rest. "The doctor and nurses say he looks okay, and he is resting quietly in a crib," I said to her. "I will go home and sleep a little bit myself and then return and spend time with you and the baby."

I had just been asleep for a short time when I received a very concerned call from the hospital saying that our newborn baby was hanging between life and death. The nurse asked, "Do you believe in infant baptism?" I rushed to the hospital. When I arrived, Susan said the nurse had brought Chad's little body in to her as though it was going to be the last time she would see him alive. As I walked into the room, we both cried and broke into a terrible noise. We decided immediately to call my parents and her family, who were people of prayer. As I look back, I realize that it was God's hope working in us to combat what was a terminal and hopeless situation.

WITHOUT HOPE, FAITH CANNOT PRODUCE A MIRACLE

In the next few hours, Chad's condition worsened so quickly that discouragement threatened to swallow up our hope. By the providence of God, one of the top neurosurgeons in the United States was a resident in our small but international community. He was called and surgery was done to remove a blood clot from Chad's brain. The X-rays showed he had three skull fractures and a major dark bruise on his brain. After the surgery Chad was taken by helicopter to Charleston, South Carolina, a ninety-minute drive away, but only a few minutes by air. The entire time that Chad was in the helicopter, he was having very severe seizures.

When the helicopter arrived, the hospital would not receive Chad. They had already informed our hospital on Hilton Head Island that they could not receive Chad, but the hospital had failed to tell the pilot. So once again the helicopter lifted off the ground to head about one hour south to Savannah, Georgia, with Chad continuing to have seizures. Everything looked hopeless in the natural, but God, by His Spirit, gave Susan and me a fighting hope.

The helicopter landed in Savannah, Georgia, with hopelessness shouting, "Chad won't make it!" But God answered the hope of our prayers and, in one week, a baby that was not expected to live, or at best was expected to live out his life in a vegetative state, went home and began to live a miraculous life.

> GROWTH+INSIGHT
>
> A fighting hope sees things as they should be, not as they are.

Today Chad is a healthy twenty-one-year-old who has played baseball and basketball most of his young life. As I write this book, Chad has graduated from Bible school and is working on another degree.

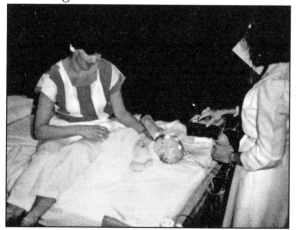

Chad with the wires attached to his head as a newborn. They said he would never make it!

What a joy to baptize my son at an early age when he accepted Jesus as his Savior. God wrought a miracle, giving us an active, vibrant son.

Chad's life has been filled with joy and pride for us as parents. What a miraculous gift God gave us.

day 18

GROWING UP MEANS LEARNING TO COPE WITH STRESS

I called on the LORD in distress; the LORD answered me and set me in a broad place. The LORD is on my side; I will not fear. What can man do to me?
—Psalm 118:5–6

The rock-strewn wilderness stretched all around him, and the chilled evening wind whipped at his flowing robe. The young man was tired and carried the look of the hunted. Unlike his twin, Esau, who happily spent weeks at a time away from the tribal tents trapping his food, Jacob was not used to the wilderness. He had always stayed close to home and meditated on the meaning of life. It was Jacob's desire for God's blessing that had led to this flight north.

His old father, Isaac, had felt that he was about to die and made it known to his favorite son, Esau, that he would impart to him the tribal blessing. Jacob wanted this blessing more than life, for it carried with it the covenant promises made by God to Abraham. Rebekah, Jacob's mother, also coveted this blessing for *her* favorite son. She loved Jacob more than she loved her husband, and together they planned to deceive Isaac.

Esau went hunting to catch his father's favorite dish to honor the occasion. While he was away, Rebekah cooked a meal she knew would satisfy Isaac, and she dressed Jacob in his brother's clothing, which had the smell of country on them. The fur of baby goats on Jacob's arms made him feel like the rough and hairy Esau. Dependent upon his senses of smell and touch since losing his sight, old Isaac was deceived and imparted the blessing to Jacob. When Esau returned, Isaac realized that he had been deceived by his wife and son and was confused and brokenhearted. Esau was full of rage and promised that as soon as Isaac died he would kill Jacob for sure.

> **GROWTH INSIGHT**
>
> Distress brings a sense of inadequacy and helplessness.

Caught in the web of lies and guilt, with a household divided against itself, Jacob fled to the north where his mother had relatives. He stumbled into the valley of Luz. The city of Luz was in the distance, but Jacob did not know how they would treat a stranger. In his fear, he curled up to sleep, with his head on a stone, shivering not only from the cold, but also from the fear of life that gripped him. He did not realize that his true spiritual destiny was about to begin. In retrospect, he called this time "the day of his distress." (See Genesis 35:3.)

Over the years, as Jacob became a rich and influential rancher, he never forgot the bloodshot eyes of Esau and his hate-filled voice promising Jacob's death. In the back of his mind, Jacob always knew he would one day have to face Esau again. When that day finally came, the Bible says, *"So Jacob was greatly afraid and distressed"* (Genesis 32:7).

The same dread and anxiety that hung heavy on Jacob's spotted life is experienced by millions today. Distress is one of America's greatest problems, and even growing Christians may live their lives feeling that they are trapped by their circumstances with no way out. Stress is the body's response to any demand, physical or emotional, and helps it maintain life. Obviously, not all stress is bad! Eating is stress; breathing is stress. Positive stress, which is motivational, is called *eustress*. However, our focus today is on negative stress, which is called *distress*. We want to find out how to handle and deal with distress, which, if left unchecked, can kill us.

> ### GROWTH INSIGHT
>
> Being distressed can be the doorway to a new life—a life we might never have found without coming to the end of our own abilities.

The original language of the Bible uses more than one word to describe the experience of distress. One of these words reflects the idea of a narrow place with no way to escape. When we feel circumstances have led us down a dead-end path, with no way out, we experience symptoms of distress. This can feel like being in a compression chamber. Enemies and adverse circumstances press in from every side to the point where we feel crushed.

If we are immature, we do not want to learn how to handle stress in God's way. We simply want the problems removed from our lives so we can continue as before. Distress brings to the surface a sense of inadequacy and helplessness. This is so uncomfortable that we shy away from it like a spooked animal. However, often this stress will not go away because God wants to use it to work maturity in our lives. Though others involved in our distress may be in the wrong, God can use them in our growing and maturing process.

When David was on the run from Saul, his original band of men came to him because they were distressed.

> *And everyone who was in distress, everyone who was in debt, and everyone who was discontented gathered to him. So he became captain over them. And there were about four hundred men with him.* (1 Samuel 22:2)

The distress was God's push toward the best that life had to offer them. And it didn't stop there! Being with David brought continually new situations of distress, but each was a stepping-stone to becoming one of David's mighty men.

As Christians, we face not only the distress common to all men, but also that caused by the hatred of the world toward those who believe in Jesus. Jesus said the road to eternal life is *"narrow."* (See Matthew 7:14.) It is the same word that is elsewhere translated *"distress."* (See Philippians 1:17 NASB; 1 Timothy 5:10 NASB, AMP; James 1:27 NASB.)

FIVE WAYS GOD USES DISTRESS

The problems you face in this life will either defeat you or strengthen and advance you in your growth process. The outcome is determined by your response to them. Unfortunately, many people fail to see how God can use adversity for good in their lives. They react foolishly and resent their circumstances, rather than pausing to consider what benefits they might bring. Here are five ways God can use distress in your life.

- **God uses distress to direct you.** Sometimes God must light a fire under you to get you moving. Problems can point us in a new direction and motivate us to change. Is God trying to get your attention? Sometimes it takes a painful situation to make us change our ways.

- **God uses distress to test you.** People are like tea bags. If you want to know what's inside them, just drop them into hot water. Has God tested your faith with distress? What does your reaction to distress reveal about you? *"My brethren, count it all joy when you fall into various trials, knowing that the testing of your faith produces patience"* (James 1:2–3).

- **God uses distress to correct you.** Some lessons you learn only through pain and failure. It's possible that when you were a child, your parents told you not to touch a hot stove, but you probably only learned that lesson by being burned. Sometimes we only learn the value of something—health, money, a relationship—by losing it. *"It is good for me that I have been afflicted, that I may learn your statutes"* (Psalm 119:71).

- **God uses distress to protect you.** A problem can be a blessing in disguise if it prevents you from being harmed by something more serious. A story is told of a man who was fired for refusing to do something unethical that his boss had asked him to do. His unemployment caused him distress, but it saved him from being convicted and sent to prison a year later when the boss's actions were eventually discovered. In the Bible, Joseph went through many hurts and problems caused by his own brothers, but at the end he was able to say to them, *"But as for you, you meant evil against me; but God meant it for good, in order to bring it about as it is this day, to save many people alive"* (Genesis 50:20).

- **God uses distress to perfect you.** Problems, when responded to correctly, are character builders. God is far more interested in your character than in your comfort. Your relationship to God and your character are the only two things you are going to take with you into eternity. *"We also glory in tribulations, knowing that tribulation produces perseverance; and perseverance, character; and character, hope"* (Romans 5:3–4).

GROWTH INSIGHT

God is at work in your life even when you do not recognize it or understand it, but it's much easier and more profitable when you cooperate with Him.

PLEASE PRAY THIS PRAYER:

Dear Father God, I come before You right now in the mighty name of Your Son, Jesus Christ. I give my life and all my circumstances of distress into Your hands today. Lord, only You can sort through all the problems and issues I am facing, so I place them all upon Your altar, that You might do with them and me what You will. I long to live for Your glory. I give all of myself to You. Do whatever You need to do to be more glorified through my life. In Jesus' name I pray these things. Amen.

IN OUR GROWING UP, DO WE SHOW GRATITUDE?

Gratitude is a major key to victory and a healing medicine for the soul. It overcomes all bitterness, complaining, and every difficult situation. The Bible teaches us to enter His gates with thanksgiving and come into His courts with praise. (See Psalm 95:2; 100:4.) Ungratefulness, as we can see from history, is the first major step to backsliding.

> *Because, although they knew God, they did not glorify Him as God, nor were thankful, but became futile in their thoughts, and their foolish hearts were darkened.*
>
> (Romans 1:21)

Are you able to thank the Lord in every situation? *"Rejoice always, pray without ceasing, in everything give thanks; for this is the will of God in Christ Jesus for you"* (1 Thessalonians 5:16–18). A thankful heart removes every negative tone, such as pessimism, criticism, or complaining. We must learn in our growth process that a thankful spirit makes us attractive to God. It delights His heart and wins His favor.

Growing up is reflected by our attitude. The attitude in which we do the will of God is as important as our obedience to Him. *"I delight to do Your will, O my God, and Your law is within my heart"* (Psalm 40:8).

> *Delight yourself also in the LORD, and He shall give you the desires of your heart.* (Psalm 37:4)

This point is well illustrated in our natural lives. A father may ask his son or daughter to do a job, but if the child obeys reluctantly or with an attitude of defiance, it brings no pleasure to the father. It is the same with our heavenly Father.

GRATITUDE AND HOSPITALITY LIVE TOGETHER

Many years ago a lady in a faded gingham dress, and her husband, dressed in a threadbare homespun suit, stepped off the train in Boston, Massachusetts, and made their way to the campus of Harvard University. They entered the outer office of the president of the university and, having no appointment, they timidly asked his secretary if they could see him. The secretary could tell in a moment that such backwoods, country hicks had no business at Harvard. She frowned at them and snapped, "He'll be busy all day." "We'll wait," the lady replied.

For hours, the secretary ignored them, hoping the couple would become discouraged and go away. They didn't. The secretary eventually grew frustrated and decided, against her better judgment, to disturb the president. "Maybe if they see you for just a few minutes they'll leave," she told him. Someone of his importance obviously didn't have the time to spend with them, but he detested gingham dresses and homespun suits cluttering up his outer office. He sighed in exasperation and, stern-faced with dignity, strutted toward the couple.

The lady told him, "We had a son who attended Harvard for one year. He loved the school and was so happy here. About a year ago he was killed in an accident. My husband and I would like to erect a memorial to him somewhere on campus."

The president wasn't touched; he was shocked. "Madam," he said gruffly, "we can't put up a statue for every person who attended Harvard and has died. If we did, this place would look like a cemetery." "Oh, no," the lady explained quickly, "we don't want to erect a statue. We thought we would like to give a building to Harvard." The president rolled his eyes, glanced at the couple, and exclaimed, "A building! Do you have any earthly idea how much a building costs? We have over seven and a half million dollars invested in the physical plant, alone." For a moment the lady was silent. The president was rather pleased with himself and thought he would finally be rid of them.

> **GROWTH INSIGHT**
>
> A thankful spirit makes us attractive to God.

The lady turned to her husband and said quietly, "Is that all it costs to start a university? Why don't we just start our own?" Her husband nodded. At this the president's face wilted in confusion. Mr. and Mrs. Leland Stanford left Harvard that day and traveled to Palo Alto, California. There they established the university that bears their name, a memorial to a son that Harvard no longer cared about.

Be hospitable to one another without grumbling.

(1 Peter 4:9)

Growing up in the grace of God leads to an increase in gratitude in your life. As you experience this in your relationships at home and on the job, you can know that God is truly doing a work of maturity in your life.

Jesus Is Our Example

And if you do good to those who do good to you, what credit is that to you? For even sinners do the same. And if you lend to those from whom you hope to receive back, what credit is that to you? For even sinners lend to sinners to receive as much back. But love your enemies, do good, and lend, hoping for nothing in return; and your reward will be great, and you will be sons of the Most High. For He is kind to the unthankful and evil. (Luke 6:33–35)

IN OUR GROWING UP, DO WE REALIZE HOW LITTLE WE KNOW?

day 20

He who has knowledge spares his words, and a man
of understanding is of a calm spirit.
—Proverbs 17:27

This verse suggests that the more we learn, the more we realize how much we do not know, and the slower we are to offer advice.

So then, my beloved brethren, let every man be swift to hear,
slow to speak, slow to wrath. (James 1:19)

Even Job, whom God called *"blameless and upright"* (Job 1:8), had to be reproved: *"Therefore Job opens his mouth in vain; he multiplies words without knowledge"* (Job 35:16). As God said to Job, He also says to us,

Who is this who darkens counsel by words without knowl-
edge? Now prepare yourself like a man; I will question you,

and you shall answer Me. Where were you when I laid the foundations of the earth? Tell Me, if you have understanding. (Job 38:2–4)

God's Word teaches us that He will unfold new revelation to us constantly for all eternity. A thorough examination of our lives will lead to an understanding that up to this time we have barely touched the surface of what God has to reveal. If we are so deceived as to think that we have arrived, then we have quit growing.

Because you say, "I am rich, have become wealthy, and have need of nothing"; and do not know that you are wretched, miserable, poor, blind, and naked; I counsel you to buy from Me gold refined in the fire, that you may be rich; and white garments, that you may be clothed, that the shame of your nakedness may not be revealed; and anoint your eyes with eye salve, that you may see. As many as I love, I rebuke and chasten. Therefore be zealous and repent. (Revelation 3:17–19)

For if anyone thinks himself to be something, when he is nothing, he deceives himself. (Galatians 6:3)

Test all things; hold fast what is good. Abstain from every form of evil. (1 Thessalonians 5:21–22)

Answer honestly the following questions about your progress on the steps to new growth and maturity in Christ:

- How well do I cope with rejection?
- How well do I respond to painful delays?
- How well do I handle failure?

- How well do I handle the loss of something?

- How well do I handle hostility sent my way?

- How well do I manage success?

Your honest answers to these questions will reveal your maturity in Christ. On day twenty of this new path of growth, it is important to realize you may not know as much about yourself as you thought you did. Make the decision today to feed upon God's Word in each of these areas so that you may progress to the next level of maturity God has for you.

IMMATURITY WILL BRING ANGER AND EMBARRASSMENT INTO YOUR LIFE

Dear Abby,

A young man from a wealthy family was about to graduate from high school. It was the custom in that affluent neighborhood for parents to give the graduate an automobile. "Bill" and his father had spent months looking at cars, and the week before graduation, they found the perfect car.

On the eve of his graduation, his father handed "Bill" a gift-wrapped Bible. He was so angry that he threw the Bible down and stormed out of the house. He and his father never saw one another again; it was only the news of his father's death that brought "Bill" back home.

As he sat one night going through his father's possessions that he was to inherit, he came across the Bible his father had given him. He brushed away the dust and opened it, only to find a cashier's check dated the day of his graduation—in the exact amount of the car they had chosen together.

—Beckah Fink, Texas

***

Dear Beckah,

I hope "Bill" read the Bible cover to cover, for it contained much that he needed to learn.

A foolish son is a grief to his father, and bitterness to her who bore him. (Proverbs 17:25)

When God Tests Us, He Shows Us How Little We Know

Now it came to pass after these things that God tested Abraham, and said to him, "Abraham!" And he said, "Here I am." Then He said, "Take now your son, your only son Isaac, whom you love, and go to the land of Moriah, and offer him there as a burnt offering on one of the mountains of which I shall tell you." (Genesis 22:1–2)

Abraham Passed the Test—Do You?

So Abraham rose early in the morning and saddled his donkey, and took two of his young men with him, and Isaac his son; and he split the wood for the burnt offering, and arose and went to the place of which God had told him....And He said, "Do not lay your hand on the lad, or do anything to him; for now I know that you fear God, since you have not withheld your son, your only son, from Me."...Then the Angel of the Lord called to Abraham a second time out of heaven, and said: "By Myself I have sworn, says the Lord, because you have done this thing, and have not withheld your son, your only son; blessing I will bless you, and multiplying I will multiply your descendants as the stars of the heaven and as the sand which is on the seashore; and your descendants shall possess the gate of their enemies. In your seed all the nations of the earth shall be blessed, because you have obeyed My voice." (Genesis 22:3, 12, 15–18)

GROWTH INSIGHT

Wisdom is obeying God even when we don't understand His ways.

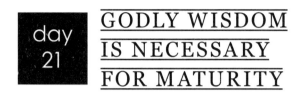

day 21

GODLY WISDOM IS NECESSARY FOR MATURITY

T he very thing that distinguishes a mature believer from an immature one is godly wisdom. *"Wisdom is the principal thing; therefore get wisdom. And in all your getting, get understanding"* (Proverbs 4:7). Wisdom will transform your childishness into discerning, growing maturity in Christ. Let me say again that Jesus Himself grew in wisdom, and as He increased in wisdom, He also grew in favor with God and man. (See Luke 2:52.)

> *And the Child grew and became strong in spirit, filled with wisdom; and the grace of God was upon Him.* (Luke 2:40)

The book of Proverbs was written to pass on wisdom from a king to a king. In fact, the theme of Proverbs is "The Making of a King." The call to each believer is to become "kingly." *"He raises the poor from the dust and lifts the beggar from the ash heap, to set them among princes and make them inherit the throne of glory"* (1 Samuel 2:8).

> *And they sang a new song, saying: "You are worthy to take the scroll, and to open its seals; for You were slain, and have*

redeemed us to God by Your blood out of every tribe and tongue and people and nation, and have made us kings and priests to our God; and we shall reign on the earth."

(Revelation 5:9–10)

Godly wisdom releases the following in your life: prudence, discernment, insight, foresight, good judgment, skill, experience, purity, peace, gentleness, and more. These "grown up" virtues are intended for success in this life and for ruling with the King of Kings in the world to come.

GROWTH INSIGHT

Godly wisdom releases the
characteristics that foster success
in this life and lead to rewards
in heaven.

On day twenty-one of this precious journey you are traveling, pray to the Lord Jesus this prayer:

Dear Lord, when I was saved, You planted Your wisdom, in seed form, in my life. Now I am determined to water it with humility and discernment. Cause it to bear fruit in me daily to bless and lead people, and to bring glory to Your name. In Jesus' name, Amen.

DO YOU HAVE THE PASSION TO FINISH STRONG?

DO YOU HAVE THE PASSION
TO FINISH STRONG?

*Not everyone who says to Me, "Lord, Lord," shall enter
the kingdom of heaven, but he who does the will of My
Father in heaven. Many will say to Me in that day, "Lord,
Lord, have we not prophesied in Your name, cast out
demons in Your name, and done many wonders in Your
name?" And then I will declare to them, "I never knew
you; depart from Me, you who practice lawlessness!"*
—Matthew 7:21–23

D epicted here is a scene of horror that will take place before Christ's white throne of judgment. On that day, all will stand before Him and give an account of their lives. Here Christ tells of those who have done mighty works for God, yet will not enter into heaven. These most miserable of all souls have tried to justify themselves by their works and have missed the entire point that all our righteousness and good works are filthy rags—unable to save us. Only Christ's sacrifice and our response to it will count on that day.

Sometimes we look at people and decide they are towers of strength and have it all together, but they may not be that way at all. Others may seem far from the ideal Christian, and we fear they will never make it into the kingdom of heaven. Yet we may be surprised on that judgment day to see them waiting for us on the other side. It is not always easy to discern how far down a person's spiritual roots go. How important it is to be rooted, grounded, strengthened, and settled, in order to endure to the end!

GODLY STRENGTH WILL HELP YOU FINISH STRONG

*But may the God of all grace, who called
us to His eternal glory by Christ Jesus,
after you have suffered a while, perfect,
establish, strengthen, and settle you.*
—1 Peter 5:10

It is important for us to understand how God evaluates a person's strength. *"He who is slow to anger is better than the mighty, and he who rules his spirit than he who takes a city"* (Proverbs 16:32). How we control our passions reveals whether, and to what degree, we are people of strength and nobility.

Samson was strong physically but weak morally. He was able to conquer a city, and he performed many miracles. However, Samson was unable to govern his own spirit. He was captive to sinful lust and self-deception. He relied on his physical strength and was brought to destruction because he neglected the things of God. By God's measure he would not qualify as a man of strength.

The two-hundred-pound weightlifter may be strong physically, but is he strong spiritually? If he cannot control his wrath or morals, if he is driven by his vices, if he is easily offended, or if he is dominated by discouragement, he is not yet a man of godly strength.

> *He does not delight in the strength of the horse; he takes no pleasure in the legs of a man. The LORD takes pleasure in those who fear Him, in those who hope in His mercy.*
>
> (Psalm 147:10–11)

DETERMINATION VERSUS FAINTHEARTEDNESS

Godly strength is the determination to accomplish God's purposes at the right time, regardless of the opposition. The unceasing efforts of the inventor Thomas Edison are the reason we have the electric light. His first attempt was to carbonize a cotton sewing thread to use as a filament. This tiny thread was carefully bent into the proper shape, laid in a nickel mold, and set in a furnace for five hours. In every case, the filament broke when Edison tried to remove it. Determined, he used an entire spool of thread. Finally he was able to mount a tiny carbon filament in a sealed bulb and pump out the air. On October 21, 1879, this prototype electric light bulb burned nonstop for nearly two hours.

> **GROWTH INSIGHT**
>
> Determination helps us overcome obstacles.

Edison said that the first requirement for success was "the ability to apply your physical and mental energies to one problem incessantly, without growing weary." It is that kind of determination that helps us overcome obstacles and provides those we lead and serve with the encouragement they need to do the same.

Godly Strength Is Measured by How We Respond to Hurt

God is against injustice, but He is more interested in our reaction to the offender than in the wrong. Our reaction reveals what is inside us, especially in our minds. God wants to reveal to us that our pride, insecurity, fear, and unforgiveness are keeping us from being strong on the inside. A person of godly strength and maturity can have a spirit-controlled temper. As we grow in wisdom, joy, peace, longsuffering, mercy, and patience, we will find ourselves responding to difficult situations as our Lord Jesus Christ did.

Godly Strength Is Marked by Initiative

Initiative has been defined as "recognizing and doing what needs to be done before I am asked to do it." Booker T. Washington was a man of initiative in his generation, working to bring academic and vocational training to former slaves. He told the following story in 1895:

A ship lost at sea for many days suddenly sighted a friendly vessel. From the mast of the unfortunate vessel was seen a signal, "Water, water; we die of thirst." The answer from the friendly vessel at once came back: "Cast down your bucket where you are." A second time the signal, "Water, water; send us water!" ran up from the distressed vessel, and was answered, "Cast down your bucket where you are." And a third and fourth signal for water was answered, "Cast down your bucket where you are." The captain of the distressed vessel, at last responding to the encouragement, cast down his bucket and it came up full of fresh sparkling water from the mouth of the Amazon River.

Washington's point was that taking initiative where you are is vital. We can look constantly to the future, but distant desires and dreams must be built on present circumstances and opportunities. Letting down the bucket is the maturity of initiative.

GODLY STRENGTH IS MARKED BY THE TESTING OF LOYALTY

We love Him because He first loved us. (1 John 4:19)

One of the best definitions of loyalty is "giving allegiance to someone when you have every right not to." This characteristic of strength, maturity, and leadership is found in the lives of two Old Testament friends, Jonathan, son of King Saul, and David, youngest son of Jesse. As they grew into early adulthood, it became evident that David would one day be given his friend Jonathan's rightful position as king of Israel. Jonathan's father, King Saul, did everything in his power to kill David because of his growing popularity. Did Jonathan side with his father's plans? No, 1 Samuel 19:1–2 says,

> *Now Saul spoke to Jonathan his son and to all his servants, that they should kill David; but Jonathan, Saul's son, delighted greatly in David. So Jonathan told David, saying, "My father Saul seeks to kill you. Therefore please be on your guard until morning, and stay in a secret place and hide."*

Not only did Jonathan warn David of the danger he was in, but he also defended David verbally when Saul was critical of him and pledged himself to David with the words, *"Whatever you yourself desire, I will do it for you"* (1 Samuel 20:4). Jonathan had learned this loyalty from David himself, not from his own father.

Consider these points:

- David had a servant's heart. Even when King Saul's heart became evil, David continued to be loyal to Saul. David understood that God had anointed Saul to be king, and he knew that if God ever wanted to remove Saul, He would do it in His timing. Until then, David would serve Saul with loyalty.

- David understood the sin of speaking against one's leader. Undermining and criticizing authority, particularly in front of others who oppose this authority, plants seeds of division and dissention. Even as a young man, David made the mature decision to let God deal with Saul's heart.

- Our growth in people skills will advance to the next level as we follow God's Word.

   Moreover if your brother sins against you, go and tell him his fault between you and him alone. If he hears you, you have gained your brother. But if he will not hear, take with you one or two more, that "by the mouth of two or three witnesses every word may be established." (Matthew 18:15–16)

- The above process of correction outlined in the Word teaches us to keep concerns private, not public, so that repentance is the goal, not disgrace. David refused to come against Saul publicly, instead showing an inner maturity beyond his physical age.

- Maturity understands that personal preference does not necessarily equal moral value. When a leader has a different style than you do, it is tempting to judge what he is doing as wrong, not just different. Even if you feel you have a better way than your leader, you need to learn that "better" is not always "right." Maturity allows for opinion and preference, rather than a judgment of right and wrong in all cases.

GROWTH INSIGHT

Leaders are often placed over us because they have something to teach us. We should thank God for their authority in our lives.

There is no doubt that Jonathan and David's deep friendship was strengthened by the testing of their loyalty. On this twenty-second day of growth, please examine your loyalty to those in authority over you and be willing to follow them even when their style of leadership differs from yours.

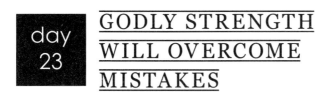

GODLY STRENGTH WILL OVERCOME MISTAKES

day 23

If you faint in the day of adversity,
your strength is small.
—Proverbs 24:10

Four Common Types of Mistakes

- **Panic-prompted Mistakes.** These mistakes are made in fear, haste, or worry. We panic and make wrong decisions.

Now there was a famine in the land and Abram went down to Egypt to dwell there, for the famine was severe in the land. And it came to pass, when he was close to entering Egypt, that he said to Sarai his wife, "Indeed I know that you are a woman of beautiful countenance. Therefore it will happen, when the Egyptians see you, that they will say, 'This is his wife'; and they will kill me, but they will let you live. Please say you are my sister, that it may be well with me for your sake, and that I may live because of you."

(Genesis 12:10–13)

Three things to note:

- ✓ We tend to trust our own devices rather than God. Whether Abram lived or not did not depend on Sarai, but on God.

- ✓ When we panic, our whole focus shifts to our circumstances and we forget that God has said, *"Do not be afraid of sudden terror, nor of trouble from the wicked when it comes; for the* Lord *will be your confidence, and will keep your foot from being caught"* (Proverbs 3:25–26).

- ✓ We tend to give more attention to what others think than to what God's Word says. For example, no age is too old to be single if God hasn't said yes. It is better to wait on God's intended for your life, than to worry that others will be critical of your single status.

- **Good Intention Mistakes.** These mistakes are made out of ignorance but with an absolutely pure motive. Moses gave us a good example in his desire to deliver the Israelites from Egypt. Moses' good intentions led to tragedy and the sin of murder. Moses thought the people would understand his intention and excuse his mistake.

Now when he was forty years old, it came into his heart to visit his brethren, the children of Israel. And seeing one of them suffer wrong, he defended and avenged him who was oppressed, and struck down the Egyptian. For he supposed that his brethren would have understood that God would deliver them by his hand, but they did not understand.

(Acts 7:23–25)

Even though he was middle-aged (seemingly old enough to know better), his attitude was, "I'll do it my way." Age has nothing to do with making mistakes. Job 32:8–9 says, *"But there is a spirit in man, and the breath of the Almighty gives him understanding. Great men are not always wise, nor do the aged always understand justice."*

- **Negligent Mistakes.** It seems that men, in particular, suffer from these mistakes of laziness or oversight.

Then Adonijah the son of Haggith exalted himself, saying, "I will be king"; and he prepared for himself chariots and horsemen, and fifty men to run before him. (And his father had not rebuked him at any time by saying, "Why have you done so?")   (1 Kings 1:5–6)

This negligence by Adonijah's father resulted in disastrous consequences.

GROWTH INSIGHT

Everyone makes mistakes. True character is revealed when a person chooses to learn from his past and move on.

Benjamin Franklin once said, "A little neglect may breed mischief: for want of a nail the shoe was lost; for want of a shoe the horse was lost; for want of a horse the rider was lost."

The soul of a lazy man desires, and has nothing; but the soul of the diligent shall be made rich. (Proverbs 13:4)

- **Blind Spot Mistakes.** These mistakes are obvious to everyone but the one making them. Double-mindedness can be caused by a blind spot mistake.

Now when Peter had come to Antioch, I withstood him to his face, because he was to be blamed; for before certain men came from James, he would eat with the Gentiles; but when they came, he withdrew and separated himself, fearing those who were of the circumcision. And the rest of the Jews also played the hypocrite with him, so that even Barnabas was carried away with their hypocrisy. But when I saw that they were not straightforward about the truth of the gospel, I said to Peter before them all, "If you, being a Jew, live in the manner of Gentiles and not as the Jews, why do you compel Gentiles to lives as Jews?" (Galatians 2:11–14)

But he who hates his brother is in darkness and walks in darkness, and does not know where he is going, because the darkness has blinded his eyes. (1 John 2:11)

God views us realistically. He knows our intentions as well as our actions, and He has no blind spots. The Word of God says,

And there is no creature hidden from His sight, but all things are naked and open to the eyes of Him to whom we must give account. Seeing then that we have a great High Priest who has passed through the heavens, Jesus the Son of God, let us hold fast our confession. (Hebrews 4:13–14)

Thanks be to God for His mercy on us, and for His restoration and reconciliation when we make those mistakes.

Do not withhold Your tender mercies from me, O LORD; let Your lovingkindness and Your truth continually preserve me. (Psalm 40:11)

For a righteous man may fall seven times and rise again, but the wicked shall fall by calamity. (Proverbs 24:16)

GROWTH INSIGHT

Failing is
not fatal
except to
the wicked!

YOUR MIND IS THE DOORWAY TO YOUR HEART AND WILL

The apostle Paul planted a church in the nation of Greece. Even though this was a highly gifted church, it was very immature. Paul had to write many encouragements and corrections to them because of their constant childishness.

> *Now I plead with you, brethren, by the name of our Lord Jesus Christ, that you all speak the same thing, and that there be no divisions among you, but that you be perfectly joined together in the same mind and in the same judgment.* (1 Corinthians 1:10)

Notice the expression Paul used here: *"the same mind."* While this referred to unity among people, an individual's mind and heart must be humbled together before God. In my life as a pastor and missionary, I have known many over the years who have a great heart but a childish mind.

Paul responded to a personal attack from the people who were supposed to be his children in the faith. This attack on Paul revealed all of their natural and spiritual immaturities.

In his second letter to the church in Corinth, Paul again tried to bring these childish Christians to a higher level of maturity through kindness and teaching.

> *For though we walk in the flesh, we do not war according to the flesh. For the weapons of our warfare are not carnal but mighty in God for pulling down strongholds, casting down arguments and every high thing that exalts itself against the knowledge of God, bringing every thought into captivity to the obedience of Christ.* (2 Corinthians 10:3–5)

GROWTH INSIGHT

God grant me the **serenity** to accept the things I cannot change, the **courage** to change the things I can, and the **wisdom** to know the difference.

Let's examine this passage further. Verse 3 says, *"We walk in the flesh."* Paul admitted he was a mortal living in the realities of the present world, but he did not war (fight) with earthly weapons. As we see in verses 4–5, our warfare is not against flesh and blood (see also Ephesians 6:12); therefore, carnal (weak, worldly) weapons will not do. We need weapons that are *"mighty in God"* (God-empowered). Their purpose is for *"pulling down"* (demolishing) strongholds (entrenched, established things that oppose God's will). Here Paul referred specifically to warfare in the mind, against arrogant, rebellious ideas and attitudes, which he called *"arguments,"* and against *"every high thing"* (pride) opposed to the true knowledge of God. The aim is to bring every disobedient thought into obedience to Christ.

Paul was teaching that the real battlefield for spiritual growth is in our minds. The psalmist gave us this good word: *"I thought about my ways, and turned my feet to Your testimonies"* (Psalm 119:59). It takes a conscious decision to examine your ways, thoughts, and attitudes to effect real spiritual growth.

GOD'S PERFECT KNOWLEDGE OF MAN

O LORD, You have searched me and known me. You know my sitting down and my rising up; You understand my thought afar off. (Psalm 139:1–2)

God knows our thoughts, but He will not change them without our inviting Him into our thought life.

When I was a child, I spoke as a child, I understood as a child, I thought as a child; but when I became a man, I put away childish things. (1 Corinthians 13:11)

Please listen to the godly advice David gave to his son Solomon, the man who is considered to be the wisest man who ever lived.

As for you, my son Solomon, know the God of your father, and serve Him with a loyal heart and with a willing mind; for the LORD searches all hearts and understands all the intent of the thoughts. If you seek Him, He will be found by you; but if you forsake Him, He will cast you off forever. (1 Chronicles 28:9)

The application is that you can have a loyal heart toward your church, your family, and toward daily responsibility, but an unwilling mind toward God. An unwilling mind will keep you from real, personal, and prosperous relationship with God. It will not respond to the voice of the heart that sees new doors of opportunity that the mind cannot see.

> *For God has not given us a spirit of fear, but of power and of love and of a sound mind.* (2 Timothy 1:7)

THE NEW MAN

> *This I say, therefore, and testify in the Lord, that you should no longer walk as the rest of the Gentiles walk, in the futility of their mind, having their understanding darkened, being alienated from the life of God, because of the ignorance that is in them, because of the blindness of their heart; who, being past feeling, have given themselves over to lewdness, to work all uncleanness with greediness* [unrestrained feelings]. *But you have not so learned Christ, if indeed you have heard Him and have been taught by Him, as the truth is in Jesus: that you put off, concerning your former conduct, the old man which grows corrupt according to the deceitful lusts, and be renewed in the spirit of your mind, and that you put on the new man which was created according to God, in true righteousness and holiness.*
>
> (Ephesians 4:17–24)

A man can be born again and love the Lord, yet have a significant need for his mind to be renewed. (See verse 23.) A major part of Christian holiness is living a life separated from the world. Jesus stressed this by saying that although we live in the world, we are not to be of the world. Be careful to identify and avoid the world's way of thinking. Realize that thinking as the world does will inevitably lead to sensuality and impurity.

> *Commit your works to the LORD, and your thoughts will be established.* (Proverbs 16:3)

GROWTH INSIGHT

We live in the world, but we are not of the world.

<table>
<tr><td>day
25</td><td>

JOY AND LAUGHTER
WILL STRENGTHEN
YOUR GROWTH

</td></tr>
</table>

W hen you begin to take major steps of growth in your relationship with God, His joy in you becomes strength.

WE WANT TO LAUGH WITH GOD, NOT AT GOD

A wonderful story is told in Genesis 17–18 of a personal visit by God to Abraham.

Then God said to Abraham, "As for Sarai your wife, you shall not call her name Sarai, but Sarah shall be her name. And I will bless her and also give you a son by her; then I will bless her, and she shall be a mother of nations; kings of peoples shall be from her." Then Abraham fell on his face and laughed, and said in his heart, "Shall a child be born to a man who is one hundred years old? And shall Sarah, who is ninety years old, bear a child?" (Genesis 17:15–17)

Then the LORD appeared to him by the terebinth trees of Mamre, as he was sitting in the tent door in the heat of the day. So he lifted his eyes and looked, and behold, three men were standing by him; and when he saw them, he ran from the tent door to meet them, and bowed himself to the ground, and said, "My Lord, if I have now found favor in Your sight, do not pass on by Your servant."...Then they said to him, "Where is Sarah your wife?" So he said, "Here, in the tent." And He said, "I will certainly return to you according to the time of life, and behold, Sarah your wife shall have a son." (Sarah was listening in the tent door which was behind him.) Now Abraham and Sarah were old, well advanced in age; and Sarah had passed the age of childbearing. Therefore Sarah laughed within herself, saying, "After I have grown old, shall I have pleasure, my lord being old also?" And the LORD said to Abraham, "Why did Sarah laugh, saying, 'Shall I surely bear a child, since I am old?' Is anything too hard for the LORD? At the appointed time I will return to you, according to the time of life, and Sarah shall have a son." But Sarah denied it, saying, "I did not laugh," for she was afraid. And He said, "No, but you did laugh!" (Genesis 18:1–3, 9–15)

Both Abraham and Sarah laughed at God because of their limited faith. This laughter reveals disbelief, not joy.

Laugh with God

Then our mouth was filled with laughter, And our tongue with singing. Then they said among the nations, "The LORD has done great things for them." The LORD has done great things for us, and we are glad. (Psalm 126:2–3)

There are times when we rejoice in the Lord that we should laugh. I believe that the Lord takes pleasure when we are so joyful that it overflows in giggles, laughter, and thigh-slapping hoots of merriment. Many people picture God as a stern task-master on high, waiting to smite His unruly creation, but if we search the Scriptures, we can see that God has a definite sense of humor.

The Humor of Christ

Elton Trueblood, the author of *The Humor of Christ,* says, "We do not know with certainty how much humor there is in Christ's teaching, but we can be sure there is far more than is normally recognized. In any case there are numerous passages in the recorded teaching which are practically incomprehensible when regarded in only a sober way, but which are humorous once we get free from the thinking that Christ never joked or laughed. When we realize that Christ was not always engaged in serious talk, we have made an enormous step on the road to understanding."

> **GROWTH INSIGHT**
>
> God has a definite sense of humor that we often overlook.

The fact is that many of us have developed a false impression of Christ's character. Though we do not always say so directly, we tend to think of Him as always mild in manner, endlessly patient, grave in speech. The evidence of this is that we may try to explain away any words or incidents in the Gospels that are inconsistent with this picture. But if we put aside this thought and "sit down before the fact as a little child," we come out with a radically different picture.

In Christ's words about being a source of light to a darkened world, He uses humor to make His point about witnessing when He asks, *"Is a lamp brought to be put under a basket or under a bed? Is it not to be set on a lampstand?"* (Mark 4:21). Since the lamp mentioned has an open flame and since the bed has a mattress, it is easy to see in this situation that the light would be suffocated or the mattress would be burned. The appeal here is to the patently absurd.

In the Gospels, Jesus is presented with many contrasting features. He is a Man of sorrows, but He is also a Man of joys; He uses firm and blunt language; He expresses blazing anger; He teases; He keeps company with a jovial crowd; He is eloquent. For example, how could we miss the fact that His words and behavior shocked His contemporaries? We are told that they were surprised that words of such grace should fall from His mouth. *"So all bore witness to Him, and marveled at the gracious words which proceeded out of His mouth. And they said, 'Is this not Joseph's son?'"* (Luke 4:22).

WHY DID SINNERS FOLLOW JESUS?

While those who had known Him found it hard to believe that Jesus was the Messiah, many heard His message, believed, and forsook their wicked ways. Why did these sinners follow Jesus? They followed Him because He had an attractive personality. He knew how to be respectfully firm, yet His whole heart was filled with love. He knew how to rejoice with His Father and laugh with people.

The fact that Christ kept company with a jovial crowd, including what the *New English Version* calls *"many bad characters,"* was extremely shocking to the religious leaders. How could there be any depth to His teaching if He failed to see how unworthy these laughing people were! *"Then all the tax collectors and the sinners drew near to Him to hear Him. And the Pharisees and scribes complained, saying, 'This Man receives sinners and eats with them"'* (Luke 15:1–2). The gospel of Mark records this story of a feast at Levi's house.

> *Now it happened, as He was dining in Levi's house, that many tax collectors and sinners also sat together with Jesus and His disciples; for there were many, and they followed Him. And when the scribes and Pharisees saw Him eating with the tax collectors and sinners, they said to His disciples, "How is it that He eats and drinks with tax collectors and sinners?"* (Mark 2:15–16)

It is clear that Christ did not fit the expected pattern. Those who followed John the Baptist, and those who were members of the Pharisaic party, engaged in sober fasts, but Christ did not do that. Both He and His disciples were noted and criticized for their eating and drinking. (See Luke 5:33–35.)

Though only His enemies called Him a drunkard, it is obvious that Christ drank wine. (Note: Wine was not considered in Jesus' day to be an alcoholic beverage. People drank wine like we drink juice. Pure and clean drinking water was hard to come by.) It was Jesus' general reputation for a good time that kept His critics after Him. If people did not like the joyful, balanced life of Christ, nor the prophetic, driven people skills of John the Baptist, what did they want?

> GROWTH INSIGHT
>
> **Christ's obvious love for all men drew sinners to Him.**

> *And the Lord said, "To what then shall I liken the men of this generation, and what are they like? They are like children*

*sitting in the marketplace calling to one another, saying:
'We played the flute for you, and you did not dance; we
mourned to you, and you did not weep.' For John the Baptist
came neither eating bread nor drinking wine, and you say,
'He has a demon.' The Son of Man has come eating and
drinking, and you say, 'Look, a glutton and a winebibber, a
friend of tax collectors and sinners!' But wisdom is justified
by all her children."* (Luke 7:31–35)

OUR GREATEST ENCOURAGEMENT TO BE JOYFUL

*A merry heart does good, like medicine, but a broken spirit
dries the bones.* (Proverbs 17:22)

A young child trying to recall this verse said, "A merry
heart doeth good like a baby aspirin." A merry heart is not
a natural state. It takes a conscious effort to keep it merry.
Joy is one of the fruits of the Spirit that needs to be cultivated. The Bible has much to say about joy and the fullness
of joy.

Rejoice in the Lord always. Again I will say, rejoice!
(Philippians 4:4)

The story is told of an elderly husband and wife who were
sitting on their front porch in rocking chairs. They had just
celebrated their sixtieth wedding anniversary. Both were talking and having a difficult time hearing one another. The husband said to his wife, "Sweetheart, you have been tried and
true all of these years." She leaned over and squinted at him
and said, "Sweetheart, I've been tired of you too all of these
years."

Joy and Laughter Will Strengthen Your Growth

A Growing Christian Is Strengthened by Joy

[Jesus said,] *"Therefore you now have sorrow; but I will see you again and your heart will rejoice, and your joy no one will take from you."* (John 16:22)

The disciples' temporary grief at their separation from Jesus, caused by His death, was replaced by the joy of a spiritual reunion through His resurrection.

Until now you have asked nothing in My name. Ask, and you will receive, that your joy may be full. (John 16:24)

Because you did not serve the LORD your God with joy and gladness of heart, for the abundance of everything, therefore you shall serve your enemies, whom the LORD will send against you, in hunger, in thirst, in nakedness, and in need of everything; and He will put a yoke of iron on your neck until He has destroyed you. (Deuteronomy 28:47–48)

Joy and a thankful heart in our lives are a priority to our God. Keep your heart full of joy and not complaints in order to grow in strength and maturity.

Though the fig tree may not blossom, nor fruit be on the vines; though the labor of the olive may fail, and the fields yield no food; though the flock may be cut off from the fold, and there be no herd in the stalls; yet I will rejoice in the LORD, I will joy in the God of my salvation. (Habakkuk 3:17–18)

To joy, rejoice, be glad, or be joyful contains the suggestion of "dancing for joy," or "leaping for joy," since the verb originally meant "to spin around with intense motion." This lays to rest the attitude that the biblical concept of joy is only a quiet inner sense of well-being. God dances for joy over Jerusalem and because of His people. (See Isaiah 65:19.)

Zephaniah 3:17 says, *"He will rejoice over you with singing."* The righteous Messiah shall rejoice in God's salvation with an intensity that the psalmist could not find words to describe. (See Psalm 21:1–2.) Also, His redeemed citizens are joyful in their King: they praise Him with dances, instruments, and singing. (See Psalm 149:2–3.) Although everything was wrong in Habakkuk's world, he leapt for joy over his fellowship with God.

ARE YOU GROWN UP ENOUGH TO LAUGH AT YOURSELF?

You will show me the path of life; in Your presence is fullness of joy; at Your right hand are pleasures forevermore.

(Psalm 16:11)

Someone has suggested that there are three degrees of laughter. The first is the laughter of a man who laughs only at his own jokes. Next is the laughter of the man who laughs at the jokes of others. The third and finest of all is the laughter of the man who laughs at himself, for this shows the precious ability to look at oneself objectively.

The story is told of a young minister who was sent to fill the pulpit of a vacationing pastor. As he drove up to the church he saw that one of the window panes had been broken out and a piece of cardboard had been placed there to keep out the weather. He said to himself, "I guess I'm like that cardboard, just placed here temporarily to keep out the weather." In the course of his message that morning, he referred to himself as that piece of cardboard. One of the parishioners, thinking to compliment the young man, remarked on the way out, "You are not like that piece of cardboard. You are a real pane."

STEALERS OF JOY

You shall laugh at destruction and famine, and you shall not be afraid of the beasts of the earth.   (Job 5:22)

When you are growing up, you are not always able to laugh at hurtful and difficult times in your life. What joy you do have in your growing up can easily be stolen by unexpected adversities. It is important to know that as we mature, we can have joy in even the most hurtful situations.

But Christ [was faithful] *as a Son over His own house, whose house we are if we hold fast the confidence and the rejoicing of the hope firm to the end.*   (Hebrews 3:6)

The key word here is *"hope."* No matter what you go through, you can always have hope that in your growing joy and relationship with Jesus, you will be protected and will come out of your adversity and hurt stronger in faith than when they entered your life.

Now may the God of hope fill you with all joy and peace in believing, that you may abound in hope by the power of the Holy Spirit.   (Romans 15:13)

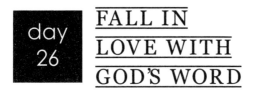

day 26
FALL IN LOVE WITH GOD'S WORD

By this twenty-sixth day of our series, you should be discovering the immaturities in your life that are hindering your growth process. The sword that will cut off every hindrance of immaturity quickly is the sword of the Spirit, which is God's Word. Ask the Holy Spirit to help you quit talking about believing God's Word and begin reading God's Word every day. You will experience supernatural growth in your life so quickly that soon you won't even recognize yourself.

> *For the word of God is living and powerful, and sharper than any two-edged sword, piercing even to the division of soul and spirit, and of joints and marrow, and is a discerner of the thoughts and intents of the heart.*
>
> (Hebrews 4:12)

You can grow only so far spiritually and emotionally without God's Word being a serious priority in your life. It is only God's Word that can strengthen you and develop your divine destiny.

Mrs. Freda Lindsay, who turned ninety-two on April 18, 2006, and who is the cofounder of the worldwide missions organization Christ For The Nations, is in her sixty-ninth time of reading the Bible through. Through her love for the Word of God, she has influenced hundreds of thousands of Christians and non-Christians in over two hundred nations. When she walks around the eighty-acre campus in Dallas, Texas, and students and visitors come toward her, she will often raise up three fingers and then five. Almost everyone on campus knows that the number three stands for reading three chapters in the Bible every day of the week and five chapters on Sunday. The three-and-five commitment will help you read the Word of God through every year.

GOD'S WORD DAILY FEEDS YOUR LIFE

Seek the LORD while He may be found, call upon Him while He is near. Let the wicked forsake his way, and the unrighteous man his thoughts; let him return to the LORD, and He will have mercy on him; and to our God, for He will abundantly pardon. "For My thoughts are not your thoughts, nor are your ways My ways," says the LORD. "For as the heavens are higher than the earth, so are My ways higher than your ways, and My thoughts than your thoughts. For as the rain comes down, and the snow from heaven, and do not return there, but water the earth, and make it bring forth and bud, that it may give seed to the sower and bread to the eater, so shall My word be that goes forth from My mouth; it shall not return to Me void, but it shall accomplish what I please, and it shall prosper in the thing for which I sent it."

(Isaiah 55:6–11)

Remember the word to Your servant, upon which You have caused me to hope. This is my comfort in my affliction, for Your word has given me life. (Psalm 119:49–50)

For whatever things were written before were written for our learning, that we through the patience and comfort of the Scriptures might have hope. (Romans 15:4)

It is vitally important to be consistent in your reading and study of God's Word. Realize that your faith will grow only as much as you feed on God's Word. Let God's Word and His Holy Spirit radically transform your way of thinking. Renew your mind to know and do the will of God, and give your body to God as a living sacrifice. (See Romans 12:1.) Recognize as a growing Christian that all sixty-six books in the Bible have a personal message for you. The old covenant lays a foundation for the new covenant in your life. Incorporate the Old Testament into your daily Bible study along with the New Testament.

GROWTH INSIGHT

Your faith will grow only as much as you feed on God's Word.

PERILOUS TIMES AND PERILOUS MEN

But know this, that in the last days perilous times will come. (2 Timothy 3:1)

Perilous means "harsh, savage, difficult, dangerous, painful, fierce, grievous, or hard to deal with." The verse describes a society that is empty of character and loose with vices and deception.

But evil men and impostors will grow worse and worse, deceiving and being deceived. But you must continue in the things which you have learned and been assured of, knowing from whom you have learned them, and that from childhood you have known the Holy Scriptures, which are able to make you wise for salvation through faith which is in Christ Jesus. All Scripture is given by inspiration of God, and is profitable for doctrine, for reproof, for correction, for instruction in righteousness, that the man of God may be complete, thoroughly equipped for every good work.

(2 Timothy 3:13–17)

The whole theme of Paul's letter to his spiritual son Timothy is that in the midst of a rebellious, deceived world, if you will stay in the Word of God, you will live in wisdom and victory. Verse 16 says that the Bible is the anointed, pure Word of God. In the middle of an

> **GROWTH INSIGHT**
>
> If you will stay in the Word of God, you will live in victory.

unsettled world, you can keep growing, and your life can make a significant difference. This verse teaches that your *"doctrine"* will get stronger. When *"reproof"* comes into your life, it means you are being tested and your new maturity is helping you to pass every test. You cannot be completely "instructed in righteousness" simply by attending your local church. Real righteousness growing in your life will only come through a personal, passionate, daily time spent in God's Word.

Your word I have hidden in my heart, that I might not sin against You! (Psalm 119:11)

GOD IS FAITHFUL TO SPEAK WHEN YOU MAKE TIME TO LISTEN

So teach us to number our days, that we may gain a heart of wisdom. (Psalm 90:12)

Every day in your life is so valuable and so important. It doesn't matter if you're a grass cutter, waitress, company president, or prime minister; the point is that everyone has only twenty-four hours in a day. Are you going to let day after day go by without developing a passionate love of reading and meditating on God's Word?

O God, You are my God; early will I seek You; my soul thirsts for You; my flesh longs for You in a dry and thirsty land where there is no water. (Psalm 63:1)

This psalm of David was written when he was in the wilderness of Judah. Instead of letting the wilderness of daily challenges, frustrations, and adversity overtake you, start your day early by reading God's Word. It will feed hope, strength, and purpose into your heart. David learned in his personal growth that the best time to spend with God was early in the morning. In the early morning, there are fewer distractions and you can give the firstfruits of your energy and focus to God and God alone. You may have many distractions in the early evening, and by the end of the day you may be too tired to spend time in God's Word.

I imagine that right now you are thinking, "How can I ever get up at 5:00 when 6:00, most of the time, is too hard. Sometimes it is so hard for me to get up at 6:00 or 6:30 to get ready to go to work that often I am running late." The answer to this is easy. Instead of staying up until 11:00, 11:30, or midnight watching TV, go to bed by 10:00 or 10:30 most of the time. Set your alarm for 4:45, and by 5:00 or 5:30 you can be in the quiet place reading God's Word.

THE PRAYER IN THE GARDEN

Even though those precious, twelve handpicked disciples loved Jesus very much, they were like many Christians today. They did not have any personal devotional discipline.

Peter said to Him, "Even if I have to die with You, I will not deny You!" And so said all the disciples. Then Jesus came with them to a place called Gethsemane, and said to the disciples, "Sit here while I go and pray over there." And He took with Him Peter and the two sons of Zebedee, and He began to be sorrowful and deeply distressed. Then He said to them, "My soul is exceedingly sorrowful, even to death. Stay here and watch with Me." He went a little farther and fell on His face, and prayed, saying, "O My Father, if it is possible, let this cup pass from Me; nevertheless, not as I will, but as You will." Then He came to the disciples and found them asleep, and said to Peter, "What? Could you not watch with Me one hour? Watch and pray, lest you enter into temptation. The spirit indeed is willing, but the flesh is weak." Again, a second time, He went away and prayed, saying, "O My Father, if this cup cannot pass away from Me unless I drink it, Your will be done." And He came and found them asleep again, for their eyes were heavy. So He left them, went away again, and prayed the third time, saying the same words. Then He came to His disciples and said to them, "Are you still sleeping and resting? Behold, the hour is at hand, and the Son of Man is being betrayed into

the hands of sinners. Rise, let us be going. See, My betrayer
is at hand." (Matthew 26:35–46)

Did the disciples lose their salvation because they slept when
Jesus needed them the most? No! But they missed a great opportunity to grow and be used by God in a difficult situation.

GROWTH INSIGHT

**If you are not awake and aware,
you may miss a great opportunity
to be used by God.**

TIME IN GOD'S WORD BRINGS SUCCESS

This Book of the Law shall not depart from your mouth, but
you shall meditate in it day and night, that you may observe
to do according to all that is written in it. For then you will
make your way prosperous, and then you will have good
success. (Joshua 1:8)

The Hebrew word for *"meditate"* indicates an active repeat-
ing of God's words. When you read His Word on a daily basis,
you begin to talk about it, understand it, and live in it.

Blessed is the man who walks not in the counsel of the un-
godly, nor stands in the path of sinners, nor sits in the seat
of the scornful; but his delight is in the law of the LORD, and
in His law he meditates day and night. He shall be like a
tree planted by the rivers of water, that brings forth its fruit
in its season. (Psalm 1:1–3)

God's Word Builds Determination to Follow Him

I have restrained my feet from every evil way, that I may keep Your word. I have not departed from Your judgments, for You Yourself have taught me. How sweet are Your words to my taste, sweeter than honey to my mouth! Through Your precepts I get understanding; therefore I hate every false way. Your word is a lamp to my feet and a light to my path.

(Psalm 119:101–105)

Can Ordinary People Understand the Bible?

Wayne Gruden, associate professor of biblical and systematic theology at Trinity Evangelical Divinity School, tells the following story:

I was scheduled to preach at a church in a village in England, and the three deacons (they had no pastor) met me before the service to pray. While we prayed, my heart was touched by the head deacon, a farmer whose prayer and conversation revealed a deep knowledge of God and a mature understanding of Scripture. Later someone told me that he had just learned to read about three years earlier! Yet prior to that time he had faithfully served as a deacon in his church and even preached frequently at other country churches. He would remember a text of Scripture, ask someone to read it to him again and again until it was firmly fixed in his mind, then meditate on it and prepare his sermon while he rode his bicycle to other village churches to preach. A few days later, I was sitting in a New Testament seminar in one of England's great

universities. Although many of the seminar participants (professors and doctoral students) had helpful
insight into the New Testament, some participants
would make comments that were so far from the
plain meaning of the text that they seemed to me to
be living proof of the fact that great intelligence and
knowledge of the Greek language do not guarantee
common sense and good judgment in understanding
Scripture. As I sat in that seminar, it struck me that if I
had a problem in my own life for which I needed guidance from Scripture, and if I had to choose between
seeking scriptural advice from that village deacon or
some of the professors or fellow students in that great
university, there is no doubt in my mind which person
I would ask. I would go to the humble deacon who
was reading his Bible in simple faith and walking with
the Lord in prayer every day. In an important way
he knew and understood Scripture better than many
people who were far more educated than he was.

David said, *"The testimony of the LORD is sure, making wise the
simple"* (Psalm 19:7). Even *"the simple"*—those who may not be
highly intelligent or educated in the world's eyes—are made
wise by God's Word. If even simple people are made wise by
Scripture, then certainly it must be true for all. God's Word is
written for everyone, not just for the highly trained experts.
The doctrine of the clarity of Scripture means that the Bible
is written in such a way that it can be understood by ordinary
people if they read it, seeking God's help in understanding it
and being willing to follow its teachings.

We see this truth confirmed in the ministry of Jesus. When people asked Him questions or made statements to put Him to the test, He never said, "I see why you have that problem—the Scriptures do not give a clear answer to that matter." No, He always put the responsibility on the people who had not read or believed Scripture as they should. Again and again He answered questions with statements like, *"Have you not read..."* (Matthew 12:3, 5; 19:4; 22:31), or *"Have you never read in the Scriptures..."* (Matthew 21:42), or even, *"You are mistaken, not knowing the Scriptures nor the power of God"* (Matthew 22:29).

GROWTH INSIGHT

God wrote the Scriptures for you!

Paul also told the Corinthians, *"For we are not writing any other things to you than what you read or understand"* (2 Corinthians 1:13).

Read it! Read it for yourself and ponder the words in your mind. God wrote it for you!

day 27
DETERMINATION CAN MAKE EVERYTHING COME TOGETHER

Then Solomon determined to build a temple for the name of the LORD, and a royal house for himself.
—2 Chronicles 2:1

Then the disciples, each according to his ability, determined to send relief to the brethren dwelling in Judea.
—Acts 11:29

For I determined not to know anything among you except Jesus Christ and Him crucified.
—1 Corinthians 2:2

But I determined this within myself, that I would not come again to you in sorrow.
—2 Corinthians 2:1

I t is clear that the key word in these verses is *"determined."*

A MATURE ATTITUDE FEEDS DETERMINATION

The attitude of gratitude is an inward feeling expressed by outward behavior. That's why your attitude can be seen without a word being spoken.

The story is told of a juvenile delinquent who was sent to a Catholic home for wayward children. As the young boy walked in the door, he told the nun he would like to have a new red bicycle. The nun said, "In your prayers tonight, if you will tell God, 'God, I'll be good for six months,' maybe He will give you a new red bicycle." That night the boy knelt beside his bed and prayed, "Dear God, I'll be good for six months if You will give me a new red bicycle." Then he said to himself, "I can never be good for six months." He started to change his prayer to two months, then one week, and finally said to himself, "I can't be good at all." While he was kneeling, he looked over and saw a statue of the Virgin Mary standing on the dresser across the room. He jumped up, ran and got it, went back to his bedside, wrapped it in a pillowcase, and stuck it under his bed. Then he prayed a new prayer, "Dear God, if You ever want to see Your mother again, You'd better give me a new red bicycle." Now that's attitude! Do you have the attitude of gratitude? Are you thankful for God's goodness?

> **GROWTH INSIGHT**
>
> You can change your attitude today and change your day.

A HEALTHY ATTITUDE DETERMINES YOUR DESTINY

The Bible supports the fact that a healthy attitude produces good results, and a poor attitude produces bad results. We can compare the apostle Paul to "doubting" Thomas. Paul said, *"I can do all things through Christ who strengthens me"* (Philippians 4:13). What did he accomplish? He wrote most of the New Testament. Where did he do most of his writing? From a dark, disease-infested jail cell. From the worst environment possible, Paul produced something that established his name and blessed the world. Two thousand years later, churches, schools, and universities are named after Paul because of his contribution, healthy attitude, and powerful determination.

"Doubting" Thomas, after following Jesus for three-and-a-half years, had a negative attitude when faced with a resurrected Christ. He had been taught by the Son of God Himself, and he had seen miracle after miracle. Yet he said, *"Unless I see in His hands the print of the nails,...and put my hand into His side, I will not believe"* (John 20:25).

DISCOURAGEMENT IS CONTAGIOUS

The story is told of a guy who was about to jump from a bridge. An alert police officer saw him and walked slowly and carefully toward the man, talking to him all the time. The policeman said, "Sir, there is absolutely no reason for you to want to jump off this bridge and kill yourself." The man turned around and said, "You don't understand; my wife has left me. My business has gone broke, and the IRS has repossessed my house." After thirty minutes of that discouraging talk, both of them jumped. Discouragement is contagious! Let one church member say it can't be done and defeat spreads like a virus.

Hope is killed by discouragement. Joy is buried by discouragement. Dreams are eaten away by the cancer of discouragement. God has more confidence in you than you have in yourself. When God made you, He put something great in you—His power of determination.

Franklin D. Roosevelt became president even though he was crippled by polio and used a wheelchair. Glen Cunningham was burned over 70 percent of his body in a schoolhouse fire and was told by his doctor that he would never walk again. He not only walked, but he was also one of the first to break the four-minute mile. If we do not live with a heart of gratitude, we cannot experience the strength of determination. One man said, "Preacher, how can I be thankful? I can't even pay my bills!" The preacher said, "Just be thankful you are not one of your creditors."

ATTITUDE IS A CHOICE

Why should we have an attitude of gratitude? Because it is a direct command of God's Word. *"Enter into His gates with thanksgiving, and into His courts with praise. Be thankful to Him, and bless His name"* (Psalm 100:4).

> **GROWTH INSIGHT**
>
> Circumstances don't determine your attitude. You do!

The young are often heard to say, "I'll be glad when I get older." Let me tell you something. Old age is not all it's cracked up to be. When you get older, many things begin to hurt, and what doesn't hurt, doesn't work. When you get to be about fifty, your hair, your teeth, and your stomach start coming out at the same time. Your knees buckle and your pants won't. Sink your teeth into a sandwich, and your teeth stay there. People say, "I'll be glad when I retire." Then you retire and that's when you get winded playing checkers. You watch the sunset if you can stay awake that long. You sit in a rocking chair, but you can't get it going. You must learn to appreciate every stage of your life and be thankful for what you have.

PRAYER IS EFFECTIVE THROUGH GRATITUDE

The attitude of gratitude is necessary to make your growing prayer life effective. *"Be anxious for nothing, but in everything by prayer and supplication, with thanksgiving, let your requests be made known to God"* (Philippians 4:6).

Without gratitude, it is a wonder God even hears us when we pray. We should follow the example set forth in the Lord's Prayer, and start our prayers with gratefulness and thanksgiving, not a series of requests and demands.

DETERMINED POWER OF ONE

In our vastly populated, impersonal world, it is easy to underestimate the significance of one. How many did it take to help the victim who got mugged on the Jericho Road? One! General Booth, founder of the Salvation Army, was *determined* that his army of believers would make a difference. Dr. Jonas Salk was *determined* to cancel out polio.

GODLY DETERMINATION OVERCOMES MOUNTAINS

The great Mount Matterhorn was never scaled until 1865. When it was first scaled by a *blind man*, he was asked, "Why did you climb to the peak of the great mountain? You knew when you arrived you could not see the view." The blind man said, "I *determined* to climb Mount Matterhorn because it was there."

Jonathan, the son of King Saul, was going through a very difficult season in his life. His father had rebelled against God and had become ineffective against the enemies of Israel. Jonathan was determined to do what was right before God. In 1 Samuel, we have a great story of godly determination being lived out in a very confusing time.

> *Now it happened one day that Jonathan the son of Saul said to the young man who bore his armor, "Come, let us go over to the Philistines' garrison that is on the other side." But he did not tell his father....Between the passes, by which Jonathan sought to go over to the Philistines' garrison, there was a sharp rock on one side and a sharp rock on the other side. And the name of one was Bozez, and the name of the other Seneh. The front of one faced northward opposite Michmash, and the other southward opposite Gibeah. Then Jonathan said to the young man who bore his armor, "Come, let us go over to the garrison of these uncircumcised; it may be that the LORD will work for us. For nothing restrains the LORD from saving by many or by few." So his armorbearer said to him, "Do all that is in your heart. Go then; here I am with you, according to your heart." Then Jonathan said, "Very well, let us cross over to these men, and we will show ourselves to them. If they say thus to us, 'Wait until we come to you,' then we will stand still in our place and not go up to them. But if they say thus, 'Come up to us,' then we will go up. For the LORD has delivered them into our hand, and this will be a sign to us." So both of them showed themselves to the garrison of the Philistines. And the Philistines said, "Look, the Hebrews are coming out of the holes where they have hidden." Then the men of the garrison called to Jonathan and his armorbearer, and said, "Come up to us, and we will show you something." Jonathan said to his armorbearer,*

*"Come up after me, for the L*ORD *has delivered them into the hand of Israel." And Jonathan climbed up on his hands and knees with his armorbearer after him; and they fell before Jonathan. And as he came after him, his armorbearer killed them. That first slaughter which Jonathan and his armorbearer made was about twenty men within about half an acre of land. And there was trembling in the camp, in the field, and among all the people. The garrison and the raiders also trembled; and the earth quaked, so that it was a very great trembling.*   (1 Samuel 14:1, 4–15)

INSIGHTS INTO JONATHAN'S DETERMINATION:

- Jonathan was *determined* to defeat the Philistines.

- Jonathan's *determination* was immediately challenged with resistance.

- No one came to stir up his *determination* or to encourage him, not even King Saul, his father.

- Jonathan had no supernatural event or prophecy that preceded this event to inspire him.

- Jonathan's mountain was filled with *"sharp rocks."* It was not an easy climb.

- Verse 13 says that Jonathan climbed up on his hands and knees. A prince who could have stayed home in his comfort zone was *determined* to do what was right, so much so that he was willing to get on his hands and knees and do what the situation called for.

- Jonathan's *determination* produced a great military victory for Israel. Look again at verses 14–15:

That first slaughter which Jonathan and his armorbearer made was about twenty men within about half an acre of land. And there was trembling in the camp, in the field, and among all the people. The garrison and the raiders also trembled; and the earth quaked, so that it was a very great trembling.

YOUR GROWING DETERMINATION SAYS:

"I'll not be beaten."

"I won't stop."

"I won't quit."

"I am determined."

GROWTH INSIGHT

In life, if you want to do anything great, anything that makes a difference, it takes holy determination.

The Bible says, *"Blessed are the peacemakers"* (Matthew 5:9). It does not say, "Blessed are the passive." Be determined to grow into a maturity that will strengthen you to press in to all that God has for you. Be determined to go to the next level of God's call on your life.

And He has made from one blood every nation of men to dwell on all the face of the earth, and has determined their preappointed times and the boundaries of their dwellings.

(Acts 17:26)

THE ART OF RESISTING THE DEVIL

Fight the good fight of faith, lay hold on eternal life, to which you were also called and have confessed the good confession in the presence of many witnesses.
—1 Timothy 6:12

J im Elliot, a missionary who was killed at an early age by the Ecuador Auca Indians, had written in his diary,

GROWTH INSIGHT

"He is no fool who gives what he cannot keep to gain what he cannot lose."

On this twenty-eighth day of change and new growth in your walk with the Lord, it is important for you to learn how to protect that growth and the new perspective your heavenly Father is giving you.

The devil and his demon spirits are at work to destroy you, and it is necessary to learn the art of resisting them. This ability is addressed in God's Word in both 1 Peter and James.

Likewise you younger people, submit yourselves to your elders. Yes, all of you be submissive to one another, and be clothed with humility, for "God resists the proud, but gives grace to the humble." Therefore humble yourselves under the mighty hand of God, that He may exalt you in due time, casting all your care upon Him, for He cares for you. Be sober, be vigilant; because your adversary the devil walks about like a roaring lion, seeking whom he may devour. Resist him, steadfast in the faith, knowing that the same sufferings are experienced by your brotherhood in the world. But may the God of all grace, who called us to His eternal glory by Christ Jesus, after you have suffered a while, perfect, establish, strengthen, and settle you. To Him be the glory and the dominion forever and ever. Amen. (1 Peter 5:5–11)

Therefore submit to God. Resist the devil and he will flee from you. (James 4:7)

Peter and James both used the word *"resist."* These men knew one another and they probably had talked about how to resist the devil and make him leave. The devil and his demons will never totally leave you alone. But each time you are attacked, if you are *"sober," "vigilant,"* and determined to *"resist,"* you can have victory in every battle.

In the *Amplified Bible,* James 4:7 says, *"So be subject to God. Resist the devil [stand firm again him], and he will flee from you."*

Important Insight:

"So be subject to God." The word *"subject"* from James 4:7 means to be under God's dominion. Habakkuk 2:4 says, *"Behold the proud, his soul is not upright in him; but the just shall live by his faith."* One of the day-to-day weaknesses many immature Christians have is that they "placate" the devil. To placate means to compromise and to make concessions. Is faith an attitude or an action in your life? One of the ways in which we disappoint God and ourselves is by substituting the attitude of faith for the act of faith. A strong and practical illustration is given to us in God's Word that clearly shows the difference between faith as an attitude or an action:

> *Now it happened, on a certain day, that He got into a boat with His disciples. And He said to them, "Let us cross over to the other side of the lake." And they launched out. But as they sailed He fell asleep. And a windstorm came down on the lake, and they were filling with water, and were in jeopardy. And they came to Him and awoke Him, saying, "Master, Master, we are perishing!" Then He arose and rebuked the wind and the raging of the water. And they ceased, and there was a calm. But He said to them, "Where is your faith?" And they were afraid, and marveled, saying to one another, "Who can this be? For He commands even the winds and water, and they obey Him!"*
>
> (Luke 8:22–25)

This day began normally for Jesus and His disciples. Suddenly they found themselves in a perilous situation. Maybe experiences like this caused Jesus to say,

The thief does not come except to steal, and to kill, and to destroy.   (John 10:10)

Sometimes in life you will find yourself in situations where you give in to the attacks of the devil. In Luke 8:25, Jesus essentially said, "Where is your faith? Where is your trust and confidence in Me, in My veracity and integrity? Where is your attitude of faith?" The disciples loved, followed, and fellowshipped with Jesus, but had not yet learned to resist the devil and to use their faith personally.

My wife, Susan, a godly mother, wife, and teacher of God's Word, has this everyday faith testimony of warfare against physical demons: For years she was challenged by TMJ, commonly known as "lockjaw." Years ago I was away on a missions trip overseas, and she was physically attacked with a locked jaw to the point where she could barely open her mouth. As she went through

> **GROWTH INSIGHT**
>
> We do not have to be broken by the devil's attacks if we respond in faith.

days of stress, prayer, and total warfare, she kept resisting the devil. One day she walked in front of the mirror, pointed at it, and said, "Devil, I am not afraid of you!" It wasn't long before her jaw unlocked. In the above Scripture, Jesus demonstrated the *attitude* of faith by His ability to sleep during the storm. Because His trust was in God, fear had no place in His life. This was an attitude of faith, but it had no effect on their predicament. When He woke up, Jesus silenced the storm and removed the danger by an act of faith.

This story focuses more on the disciples' lack of faith than on Jesus' power. When the storm left, He said, *"Where is your faith?"* This seems to indicate that Jesus was surprised at their failure to believe.

TRUTHS TO UNDERSTAND

Jesus wanted the disciples to move into an attitude of faith that would activate acts of faith.

I believe Jesus is often saying to us in the storms of life, "Where is your faith?"

God wants us to learn how to resist the devil, the enemy of our souls. The apostle Paul taught, *"Do not...give place to the devil"* (Ephesians 4:26–27). The *Amplified* version of this Scripture says, *"Leave no [such] room or foothold for the devil [give no opportunity to him]."*

Stand firm against the schemes of the devil.

(Ephesians 6:11 NASB)

To *"stand"* is the act of stepping or staying in one place. A halt for defense or resistance. A strongly or aggressively held position on a debatable problem. The place taken by a witness for testifying in court.

To be *"firm"* is to be securely or solidly fixed in place. Not weak or uncertain. Not subject to change or revision, not easily moved or disturbed, "steadfast."

Paul, the great New Testament warrior, continued to teach the Ephesian church how to resist the devil. We must think our salvation through. If we do not learn how to resist the devil, he will keep stealing any effective ministry and growth we have made. Let's take a close look at Ephesians 6:10–13.

"Finally, my brethren, be strong in the Lord and in the power of His might" (verse 10). *"Finally"* does not imply a "conclusion," but an attitude for the rest of our lives and their challenges and concerns.

> *Put on the whole armor of God* [the armor of a heavily armed soldier], *that you may be able to stand against the wiles of the devil.*   (verse 11)

The *Amplified* version says, *"That you may be able successfully to stand up against [all] the strategies and the deceits of the devil."*

> *For we do not wrestle against flesh and blood, but against principalities, against powers, against the rulers of the darkness of this age, against spiritual hosts of wickedness in the heavenly places. Therefore take up the whole armor of God, that you may be able to withstand in the evil day, and having done all, to stand.*   (verses 12–13)

The verb *"withstand"* suggests vigorously opposing, bravely resisting, standing face-to-face against an adversary. With the authority and spiritual weapons given to us, we can *"withstand"* any evil force, sickness, disease, sin, hurt, or rejection. But if we don't have a resolution (determination) to stand, weapons are useless.

LEARNING TO RESIST AND ENDURE

Second Timothy reflects the horrible predicament Timothy was facing as a Christian. Thousands of his brothers and sisters in the Lord were being slain by Emperor Nero. Their battle zone was real, and many died a premature death by means of torture. Satan was enraged that Jesus had been raised from the dead! With all of his fury, he released the power of hell against the church! Even *children* who professed to know Christ were being killed for their faith. Nevertheless, the gates of hell did not prevail against the church!

We have a letter written by a Roman governor to a subsequent emperor, Trajan, that says, in effect, "I do not know just what to do with the Christians, for I have never been present at one of their trials. Shall I punish boys and girls as severely as grownups? Is just being a Christian enough to punish or must something bad actually be done? If the accused says he is not a Christian, shall I let him go? What I have done in the case of those who admitted they were Christians was to order them sent to Rome, if citizens, and if not, to have them killed. I was sure they deserved to be punished because they were so stubborn. I gave them three chances to save themselves by putting incense on your altar [speaking to the emperor] and cursing Christ."

> **GROWTH INSIGHT**
>
> Would someone find enough evidence to convict you of being a Christian?

In his letter, this governor mentioned what he had heard about Christians. He wrote, "I have heard that a real Christian will not do this [renounce Christ or offer incense]. The Christians claim that they do nothing worse than meet before dawn on a certain day and sing hymns to their Christ. They promise not to steal or lie. They also meet for a common meal [this was

THE ART OF RESISTING THE DEVIL

the Lord's Supper or communion], though they haven't given it up since my order against secret meetings. I have had some women called deaconesses tortured, but could not find out anything worse than some crazy teachings and ideas. Many people had previously been touched by this foolishness and the temples were nearly empty. But now [since the persecution became so intense] the people are coming back to the temple again."

The most famous example of Christian martyrdom is undoubtedly that of an eighty-six-year-old brother in the Lord, Polycarp, Bishop of Smyrna. His martyrdom occurred 150 years after the death and resurrection of Jesus, and indicates that the fervor against Christians was increasing with time.

> **GROWTH INSIGHT**
>
> If your faith isn't worth dying for, what are you living for?

The story is that, during a huge gathering of pagans, the mob began screaming, "Away with the atheists!" (This was what they called the Christians, because the Christians refused to burn incense to pagan gods.)

Suddenly, in the midst of the growing riot, someone yelled, "Get Polycarp!" Polycarp, unafraid of death, wanted to surrender, but other believers persuaded him at first to hide in the country.

After Polycarp was discovered, a government official who was related to another Christian looked into the old man's eyes and asked him, "What is the harm in saying, 'Caesar is Lord,' and putting incense on his altar and saving yourself?" Polycarp strongly refused.

Then the governor gave Polycarp three chances to save himself from being thrown to the lions in the great arena. After Polycarp refused the first two chances, the governor spoke to him again and said, "Renounce Christ!"

Polycarp answered, "Eighty and six years have I served Him, and He has done me no wrong, and can I revile my King that saved me?"

The governor insisted again, "Swear by Caesar! I'll throw you to the beasts if you do not!" The old bishop answered, "Bring on the beasts!"

> **GROWTH INSIGHT**
>
> "Get a hold on the devil when he first attacks."
> —Gordon Lindsay

The governor quickly replied with indignation, "If you scorn the beasts, I'll have you burned!" Polycarp looked him straight in the eyes and said, "You try to frighten me with the fire that burns for an hour and you forget the fire of hell that never goes out."

Infuriated by Polycarp's boldness, the governor yelled to the crowd, "Polycarp admits he is a Christian!" The crowd went wild, hollering and shouting. They said, "This is the teacher of Asia, the father of Christians, the destroyer of our gods."

The crowd then got huge bundles of wood and placed them around the feet of the faithful bishop. As the fire began to burn his flesh, tradition says that Polycarp prayed loudly, "Lord God Almighty, Father of Jesus Christ, I bless Thee that Thou didst deem me worthy of this hour, that I shall take a part among the martyrs in the cup of Christ and to rise again with the power of the Holy Spirit. May I be an acceptable sacrifice. I praise Thee. I bless Thee. I glorify Thee through Jesus Christ."

> *For whatever is born of God overcomes the world. And this is the victory that has overcome the world; our faith. Who is he who overcomes the world, but he who believes that Jesus is the Son of God?* (1 John 5:4–5)

> *Therefore, my beloved brethren, be steadfast, immovable, always abounding in the work of the Lord, knowing that your labor is not in vain in the Lord.* (1 Corinthians 15:58)

Resisting the devil is not simply ignoring him. You must be alert and recognize when he is trying to lay hold on your life in some form or manner. Then push him back consistently by speaking to him in the name of Jesus.

BIBLICAL FASTING, THE DOOR TO CONSISTENT VICTORY

Moreover, when you fast, do not be like the hypocrites, with a sad countenance. For they disfigure their faces that they may appear to men to be fasting. Assuredly, I say to you, they have their reward. But you, when you fast, anoint your head and wash your face, so that you do not appear to men to be fasting, but to your Father who is in the secret place; and your Father who sees in secret will reward you openly.
—Matthew 6:16–18

Fasting is a gift from God that is rarely used by Christians today. Fasting on a regular basis is like exercise. Similar to working out, it brings strength to your spirit and certainly can be a high mark of Christian maturity in your life. Mark's gospel tells a good story about how Jesus taught His disciples the significance and power of prayer and fasting.

And when He came to the disciples, He saw a great multitude around them, and scribes disputing with them. Immediately, when they saw Him, all the people were greatly amazed, and running to Him, greeted Him. And He asked the scribes, "What are you discussing with them?" Then one of the crowd answered and said, "Teacher, I brought You my son, who has a mute spirit. And wherever it seizes him, it throws him down; he foams at the mouth, gnashes his teeth, and becomes rigid. So I spoke to Your disciples, that they should cast it out, but they could not." He answered him and said, "O faithless generation, how long shall I be with you? How long shall I bear with you? Bring him to Me." Then they brought him to Him. And when he saw Him, immediately the spirit convulsed him, and he fell on the ground and wallowed, foaming at the mouth. So He asked his father, "How long has this been happening to him?" And he said, "From childhood. And often he has thrown him both into the fire and into the water to destroy him. But if You can do anything, have compassion on us and help us." Jesus said to him, "If you can believe, all things are possible to him who believes." Immediately the father of the child cried out and said with tears, "Lord, I believe; help my unbelief!" When Jesus saw that the people came running together, He rebuked the unclean spirit, saying to it, "Deaf and dumb spirit, I command you, come out of him and enter him no more!" Then the spirit cried out, convulsed him greatly, and came out of him. And he became as one dead, so that many said, "He is dead." But Jesus took him by the hand and lifted him up, and he arose. And when He had come into the house, His disciples asked Him privately, "Why could we not cast it out?" So He said to them, "This kind can come out by nothing but prayer and fasting." (Mark 9:14–29)

Again, fasting is a hidden weapon that has largely been lost to the church over the last few centuries, but we need to know that it is one of the greatest weapons God has given to His end-time army.

Just a short time before the incident in Mark, Jesus had commissioned His disciples and given them authority over all unclean spirits and sickness. *"And when He had called His twelve disciples to Him, He gave them power over unclean spirits, to cast them out, and to heal all kinds of sickness and all kinds of disease"* (Matthew 10:1). But as we have seen in Mark 9, our key text, these disciples had run into a solid wall of evil that just wouldn't move for them. This obstacle prevented the disciples from bringing deliverance and freedom to this family.

> **GROWTH INSIGHT**
>
> Certain victories will never be won unless we partner our prayers with fasting.

Was the authority Jesus had given the disciples still there? Yes! Jesus had given them spiritual authority to cast out devils, but for some reason they had run into a new type of demonic force, a force that would not yield to the level of anointing and growth they had in their lives.

Jesus pointed out that some demons (strongholds) are stronger than others, and we must be adequately prepared to engage in spiritual battles. The implication was that the disciples failed to deliver this precious boy because of their unbelief.

So He said to them, "This kind can come out by nothing but prayer and fasting." (Mark 9:29)

There will be times in your life when you will be stopped or greatly hindered by obstructions such as...

- A demonic power
- Unforgiveness
- Iniquity—a specific sin that returns again and again.

These obstructions will not budge until you combine your prayers with fasting. Fasting increases the power and intensity of your prayers exponentially.

PURPOSES OF FASTING:

To Chasten the Soul

When I wept and chastened my soul with fasting, that became my reproach. (Psalm 69:10)

To Humble the Soul

Then I proclaimed a fast there at the river of Ahava, that we might humble ourselves before our God, to seek from Him the right way for us and our little ones and all our possessions. (Ezra 8:21)

To Seek the Lord

And Jehoshaphat feared, and set himself to seek the LORD, and proclaimed a fast throughout all Judah. So Judah gathered together to ask help from the LORD; and from all the cities of Judah they came to seek the LORD.

(2 Chronicles 20:3–4)

31 DAYS OF SPIRITUAL GROWTH

For Communion with Christ

And Jesus said to them, "Can the friends of the bridegroom mourn as long as the bridegroom is with them? But the days will come when the bridegroom will be taken away from them, and then they will fast."   (Matthew 9:15)

For Protection in Danger

Then Esther told them to reply to Mordecai: "Go, gather all the Jews who are present in Shushan, and fast for me; neither eat nor drink for three days, night or day. My maids and I will fast likewise. And so I will go to the king, which is against the law; and if I perish, I perish!"   (Esther 4:15–16)

Blessing Connected to Fasting

Thus says the LORD of hosts: "The fast of the fourth month, the fast of the fifth, the fast of the seventh, and the fast of the tenth, shall be joy and gladness and cheerful feasts for the house of Judah. Therefore love truth and peace."

(Zechariah 8:19)

LENGTH OF FASTS:

Part of a Day

Now the king went to his palace and spent the night fasting; and no musicians were brought before him. Also his sleep went from him.   (Daniel 6:18)

One Day

Now on the twenty-fourth day of this month the children of Israel were assembled with fasting, in sackcloth, and with dust on their heads.   (Nehemiah 9:1)

Longer Than One Day

As you continue to seek the truth with regard to fasting, you will find that the Bible clearly mentions three-, seven-, and twenty-one-day fasts. (See Ezra 10:6–8; Esther 4:16; Acts 9:9; 1 Samuel 31:13; and Daniel 10:3.) Before you get into fasts of three weeks or more, you need to have developed this practice over time. Even if you have been fasting for shorter terms on a regular basis, these longer fasts need to be shared with your family and leaders for proper covering and medical wisdom.

A Brief History of Fasting

Christians who accept the invitation to fast have the unique privilege of identifying with some of the great heroes of the faith throughout the ages. In the Old and New Testaments, fasting was the practice of self-denial.

Many scholars believe that the practice of fasting began with the loss of appetite during times of great distress. Hannah, who would later become the mother of Samuel, was so distressed about her inability to have children that she *"wept and did not eat"* (1 Samuel 1:7). Other Old Testament passages share the same insight. It seems that fasting was most often a response to deep grief.

Fasting Will Bring Growing Insight

Adam and Eve's disobedience in the garden of Eden was the original cause of man's losing his God-given dominion. Jesus fasted for forty days and forty nights in the wilderness and overcame the fiercest attacks the enemy could bring. These were more than just little temptations in the wilderness;

they were major hits by Satan on Jesus. Jesus' restraint made possible the restoration of our dominion in daily life.

Adam and Eve had the Garden of Eden as their home with the freedom to enjoy everything and to eat everything except the fruit of the Tree of Knowledge of Good and Evil. But when Eve saw that the tree was *"good for food"* and *"pleasant to the eyes"* (Genesis 3:6), she and her husband, by eating it, released the spirit of sin on the human race. Christ, the second Adam, by refusing to turn stones into bread at the devil's suggestion, completed His fast and won back the battle that was lost by Adam and Eve.

> **GROWTH INSIGHT**
>
> Fasting is the process by which the impossible becomes possible.

In Genesis, Esau sold his birthright for a bowl of soup. When our appetites are uncontrolled, this leads to spiritual dryness and many times to spiritual disaster. Esau should have been the father of the chosen race instead of Jacob. Esau was the oldest of twins and the birthright was rightfully his. Yet, there was one fundamental difference between Esau and Jacob. Jacob had wisdom and understood the value of the birthright; Esau was a man of the earth and he thought only in terms of the now.

> *And Esau said to Jacob, "Please feed me with that same red stew, for I am weary." Therefore his name was called Edom. But Jacob said, "Sell me your birthright as of this day." And Esau said, "Look, I am about to die; so what is this birthright to me?" Then Jacob said, "Swear to me as of this day." So he swore to him, and sold his birthright to Jacob. And*

Jacob gave Esau bread and stew of lentils; then he ate and drank, arose, and went his way. Thus Esau despised his birthright. (Genesis 25:30–34)

All through the Scriptures, we find men losing their places with God through a failure to control the temptations of the flesh. In contrast, we find others who, through the discipline of fasting, overcame all obstacles, getting answers from God and fulfilling their destinies.

AVOID PERSONAL PRIDE IN FASTING

To exalt fasting as a means of satisfying personal ambition or pride is wrong. An example of someone who boasted of his fasting was the Pharisee in Luke 18:11–14.

The Pharisee stood and prayed thus with himself, "I fast twice a week; I give tithes of all that I possess." And the tax collector, standing afar off would not so much as raise his eyes to heaven, but beat his breast, saying, "God, be merciful to me a sinner!" I tell you, this man went down to his house justified rather than the other; for everyone who exalts himself will be humbled, and he who humbles himself will be exalted.

The physical purpose of fasting is the denial and discipline of the body so that it is submitted to God. The divine purpose of fasting is to strengthen the faith of those who seek to bring God's kingdom on earth, to bring deliverance to the sick, the sinner, and the heavy burdened.

GOING THE DISTANCE AND FINISHING STRONG

I have fought the good fight,
I have finished the race, I have kept the faith.
—2 Timothy 4:7

IF YOU DON'T DARE TO GO TOO FAR, YOU WON'T KNOW HOW FAR YOU CAN GO!

The year 1994 was a great year for the National Basketball Association draft. There were three rookies destined for greatness who came out of the NBA draft that year. One of them was Grant Hill, another was Jason Kidd, and the third was Glenn Robinson. Now, it is very rare that there are three drafted in one year who have the ability to single-handedly turn a franchise around just by their personal talent.

These three men were franchise players. Grant Hill impacted Detroit (along with signing a $70 million shoe contract); Jason Kidd, the Dallas Mavericks; and Glenn Robinson made Milwaukee a contender overnight. All three of these men had the potential and anointing in their world to impact both a team and a city.

The year 1954 was a great year for rookie evangelists. Three young men came on the scene that year. They were dynamic and powerful preachers. Their names were Billy Graham, Ron Clifford, and Chuck Templeton. Now, most would say, "I know of Billy Graham, but Ron Clifford and Chuck Templeton? Who in the world are they?"

Let me tell you first about Chuck Templeton. He was brilliant; in fact, some said he was the greatest preacher of his day. *Time* magazine wrote an article that said it was believed he would be the Babe Ruth of evangelism.

Ron Clifford, a great southern evangelist, came out of the chute like a wild bull. Some said he was the greatest preacher in the world. Other preachers clamored around him. People in high places always wanted to be with him. He was handsome, intelligent, and a gifted speaker. Once, when he spoke at Baylor University in Waco,

> **GROWTH INSIGHT**
>
> We need to keep our focus if we want to finish the race strong.

Texas, they actually cut the ropes of the bell tower so no one would be disturbed while he preached. This man was so dynamic and powerful that when they made the movie *The Robe* in Hollywood, they sent for Ron Clifford to play the leading role. Yet we never hear of Ron Clifford or Chuck Templeton. We only know of Billy Graham. Why?

By the age of thirty-five, Ron Clifford had divorced his wife, forsaken his three mentally handicapped children, and died of cirrhosis of the liver. In 1959, Chuck Templeton stunned the world by announcing he was quitting the ministry and was going to be an announcer in Canada. He no longer believed that Jesus Christ was the Son of God. He became a devout atheist.

But we have all heard of Billy Graham. His crusades have brough the message of the good news of Jesus Christ to millions of people around the world. Why do I bring these stories to your attention? Because it reinforces the importance of finishing strong in the race of life.

And because lawlessness will abound, the love of many will grow cold. But he who endures to the end shall be saved.
(Matthew 24:12–13)

If you faint in the day of adversity, your strength is small.
(Proverbs 24:10)

STRIVING FOR A CROWN

Do you not know that those who run in a race all run, but one receives the prize? Run in such a way that you may obtain it. And everyone who competes for the prize is temperate in all things. Now they do it to obtain a perishable crown, but we for an imperishable crown. Therefore I run thus; not with uncertainty. Thus I fight: not as one who beats the air. But I discipline my body and bring it into subjection, lest, when I have preached to others, I myself should become disqualified. (1 Corinthians 9:24–27)

Athletes who break the rules become disqualified. Paul's illustration stresses the necessity of self-discipline and the danger of losing focus.

Paul said in verse 26, *"Therefore I run thus: not with uncertainty."* When you watch Olympic runners, there is a certain way—a rhythm—in which they run. It is easy to lose your rhythm or focus even in doing good things. Verse 24 says, *"Run in such a way that you may obtain it."*

> *Therefore we also, since we are surrounded by so great a cloud of witnesses, let us lay aside every weight, and the sin which so easily ensnares us, and let us run with endurance the race that is set before us.* (Hebrews 12:1)

> *But [like a boxer] I buffet my body [handle it roughly, discipline it by hardships] and subdue it, for fear that after proclaiming to others the Gospel and things pertaining to it, I myself should become unfit [not stand the test, be unapproved and rejected as a counterfeit].* (1 Corinthians 9:27 AMP)

TRAIN TO WIN

> *Do you not know that those who run in a race all run, but one receives the prize? Run in such a way that you may obtain it.* (1 Corinthians 9:24)

For the Olympics, they don't just get people off the street. Can't you just see someone one week before the race being dragged off the street? Someone just walking around as the Olympic coach drives up in his car. "Hey you! Would you be interested in running in the Olympics next week?" "Yes, I would," is the response, "but what would I have to do?" The coach holds something up from the front seat. "Oh, just wear these skinny, little shorts, these shoes, and this tank top. A week from today show up here at about 8:00 a.m. Go to the athletics door and a security man will let you in. Then run out onto the track with the other runners and when the sound of the gun goes off, you start running. You're going to run until you see the taped finish line, and if you break the tape first, we are going to put your face and name on a Wheaties box." That's not how it works. Runners prepare to win from a very young age and at a great price.

GROWTH INSIGHT

"One must know the value of the prize and be willing to pay the price."
—Freda Lindsay

Have you ever watched a marathon? There is a world of difference between the way marathon athletes run and the way you and I do. Marathon runners *sleep* faster than we run! When they run that twenty-six mile race, they are putting down five-minute miles. Can you imagine those grueling miles? They don't just decide one day to run and win; they have trained and trained. They are in the race to win. If we do not go the distance, if we do not finish strong, it may be because we have not trained to win.

MISTAKEN BELIEFS OF GROWING CHRISTIANS

- The Holy Spirit will always help me. It doesn't matter how I live between Sundays.

- My attendance at church is all I need to make it to the finish line strong.

It's the growing spiritual passion in you, coupled with the responsibility of self-discipline, that ensures a strong finish.

HAVE A PLAN

Therefore I run thus: not with uncertainty.

(1 Corinthians 9:26)

Paul meant, "I have a plan, a strategy, in my running. I'm conditioning myself as I work hard every day. Even when I'm having bad days, I'm training myself to finish the race strong."

• Disadvantages do not disqualify you.

Everyone has some kind of disadvantage—spiritual, emotional, physical—past or present. Tom Sullivan was a part of the 1958 U.S. Olympic wrestling team. His team did not win a gold medal, but it had to feel good just to get that far.

Tom Sullivan was a runner, swimmer, and sky-diver—a high-energy person. He was also born without eyeballs. He had two glass eyes, and sometimes when he wrestled he used this *disadvantage* as an *advantage*. If Tom was pinned on his back by his wrestling opponent, he would often pop out his fake eyes to distract his opponent long enough to get free.

As you run this race your disadvantages can become your advantages. The Word says in 2 Corinthians 12:9 that God's strength is made perfect in our weakness. Helen Keller was once asked what would be worse than being born blind. She quickly answered, "To have sight and no vision."

- We are incapable of telling a good day from a bad day.

  It looked like a bad day when Joseph was sold into slavery. It looked like a bad day when Potiphar's wife lied about Joseph. It looked like a bad day when Joseph went to jail. It looked like a bad day when the chief butler forgot Joseph in jail. Yet time revealed they were all good days, because they were all part of God's plan.

- Adversity is your best friend.

When all kinds of trials and temptations crowd into your lives, my brothers, don't resent them as intruders, but welcome them as friends! Realize that they come to test your faith and to produce in you the quality of endurance. But let the process go on until that endurance is fully developed and you will find you have become men of mature character, men of integrity, with no weak spots.

(James 1:2–4 PHILLIPS)

That's finishing strong! Adversity is God's gift to work endurance in our lives. Too often our prayers have been, "Deliver me quickly." The Lord says, "No, I will visit you in your fiery furnace." We often want God to work in us apart from adversity, when adversity is our best opportunity for growth. God wants to visit us in our fire and walk us through it for His greater glory.

It is good for me that I have been afflicted, that I may learn your statutes....I know, O Lord, that Your judgments are right, and that in faithfulness You have afflicted me.

(Psalm 119:71, 75)

- It is possible to learn to survive the ambushes of life.

"Be watchful in all things" (2 Timothy 4:5). Some ambushes may be the inability to discern spiritually the advice you are given or neglected prayer.

Getting through ambushes is what separates strong finishers who go the distance from those who drop out. Mature Christians survive the ambushes by anticipating them.

RUNNING AN EXTRA DAY FOR MORE STRENGTH

When you want to develop physical strength you often must do extra things to get where you want to go. The same principle applies to your spiritual and emotional growth. In fact, you have to keep growing the rest of your life to build the passion that will carry you to a strong finish.

> *Brethren, I do not count myself to have apprehended; but one thing I do, forgetting those things which are behind and reaching forward to those things which are ahead, I press toward the goal for the prize of the upward call of God in Christ Jesus.* (Philippians 3:13–14)

> *According to the grace of God which was given to me, as a wise master builder I have laid the foundation, and another builds on it. But let each one take heed how he builds on it. For no other foundation can anyone lay than that which is laid, which is Jesus Christ. Now if anyone builds on this foundation with gold, silver, precious stones, wood, hay,*

*straw, each one's work will become clear...of what sort it is.
If anyone's work which he has built on it endures, he will
receive a reward. If anyone's work is burned, he will suffer
loss; but he himself will be saved, yet so as through fire.*
(1 Corinthians 3:10–15)

This chapter is an extra growth day for your total victory.

ENCOUNTERING THE CHRIST OF REVELATION

In these days of political correctness and seeker-friendly
church services, we rarely hear of Jesus mentioned as a judge.
If you have ever been in a courtroom with people who were
standing before a judge, you know how sobering it is.

*Then I turned to see the voice that spoke with me. And hav-
ing turned I saw seven golden lampstands, and in the midst
of the seven lampstands One like the Son of Man, clothed
with a garment down to the feet and girded about the chest
with a golden band. His head and hair were white like wool,
as white as snow, and His eyes like a flame of fire; His feet
were like fine brass, as if refined in a furnace, and His voice
as the sound of many waters.* (Revelation 1:12–15)

Jesus' presence in this Scripture was awesome and terrify-
ing, and He was apparently wearing a judge's robe. Are you
preparing for that day when you will stand face-to-face before
your Lord, the judge of the earth? Is your growth in Christ
guiding you to lay up treasure in heaven? A fire is coming in
your life that will test what you have added to the foundation
of your salvation. The judgment seat of Christ is only for true
Christians, and the purpose of the judgment seat of Christ in

your future is not to punish sin. God will be looking for things in your life to reward. Will the things you have built survive the Refiner's fire?

> *Then I saw a great white throne and Him who sat on it, from whose face the earth and the heaven fled away. And there was found no place for them. And I saw the dead, small and great, standing before God, and books were opened. And another book was opened, which is the Book of Life. And the dead were judged according to their works, by the things which were written in the books. The sea gave up the dead who were in it, and Death and Hades delivered up the dead who were in them. And they were judged, each one according to his works. Then Death and Hades were cast into the lake of fire. This is the second death. And anyone not found written in the Book of Life was cast into the lake of fire.*
> (Revelation 20:11–15)

The Bible is teaching us that everyone on earth will be called to judgment for the choices they have made.

> *Let us hear the conclusion of the whole matter: Fear God and keep His commandments, for this is man's all. For God will bring every work into judgment, including every secret thing, whether good or evil.* (Ecclesiastes 12:13–14)

There are blessings and rewards for the saved and terrible judgment and punishment for the lost.

> *But woe to you, scribes and Pharisees, hypocrites! For you shut up the kingdom of heaven against men; for you neither go in yourselves, nor do you allow those who are entering to go in.* (Matthew 23:13)

WHERE WILL YOU STAND ON JUDGMENT DAY?

Therefore we make it our aim, whether present or absent, to be well pleasing to Him. For we must all appear before the judgment seat of Christ, that each one may receive the things done in the body, according to what he has done, whether good or bad. (2 Corinthians 5:9–10)

Four and a half centuries ago, Martin Luther said that on his calendar there were two days: Today and That Day. He realized that all of the days of his life on earth were total preparation for that sobering day when he would stand before God in eternity and give an account for his life.

In his first letter to the Corinthian church, Paul presented this important insight, which can strengthen your growth and maturity: *"Therefore judge nothing before the time, until the Lord comes, who will both bring to light the hidden things of darkness and reveal the counsels of the hearts. Then each one's praise will come from God"* (1 Corinthians 4:5). As you continue to grow and run the race of life, God will be looking for the fruits of Christ's righteousness in your life.

Missionaries Rodney and Ellie Hein, from Zimbabwe, Africa, shared this story. "Every morning in Africa a gazelle wakes up. It knows it must run faster than the fastest lion or it will be killed....Every morning a lion wakes up. It knows it must outrun the slowest gazelle or it will starve to death. It doesn't matter if you are a lion or a gazelle....When the sun comes up, you'd better be running."

Each one of us will be judged on that final day. Where will you stand and what will remain?

And this I pray, that your love may abound still more and more in knowledge and all discernment, that you may approve the things that are excellent, that you may be sincere and without offense till the day of Christ.

(Philippians 1:9–10)

Paul intended for the Philippians' love to result in their ability both to discern and to choose what is morally best.

Test all things; hold fast what is good. Abstain from every form of evil. (1 Thessalonians 5:21–22)

In our passionate desire to grow, go the distance, and finish strong, it is good for us to know, *"God resists the proud, but gives grace to the humble"* (1 Peter 5:5). Humility is foundational to spiritual strength in a growing life, just as careful natural eating is foundational to physical strength. *"Also He spoke this parable to some who trusted in themselves that they were righteous, and despised others"* (Luke 18:9). You cannot grow in your relationship with God by being a faultfinder toward others.

> **GROWTH INSIGHT**
>
> Christ never condemned sinners. He condemned hypocrites.

In the first three chapters of Revelation, Jesus did not tell the seven churches they were perfect in His eyes. He revealed to them their hearts by pointing out their sins. He challenged them to be overcomers to the end. Each church had unique and difficult troubles, but in God's heart they were to keep running the race to finish strong.

A Growing Passion Keeps Your Heart Clean

The heart is deceitful above all things, and desperately wicked; who can know it? (Jeremiah 17:9)

Who can understand his errors? Cleanse me from secret faults. Keep back Your servant also from presumptuous sins; let them not have dominion over me. Then I shall be blameless, and I shall be innocent of great transgression. (Psalm 19:12–13)

Love the Truth

The strongest spiritual medicine you can ever take is to love truth. When you love truth, regardless of how many hurts and bumps you receive in the race, you will quickly heal. Your passion for spiritual growth will keep you on the track of life. You will go the distance, and finish strong.

FINISHING STRONG

Elisha had become sick with the illness of which he would die. Then Joash the king of Israel came down to him, and wept over his face, and said, "O my father, my father, the chariots of Israel and their horsemen!" And Elisha said to him, "Take a bow and some arrows." So he took himself a bow and some arrows. Then he said to the king of Israel, "Put your hand on the bow." So he put his hand on it, and Elisha put his hands on the king's hands. And he said, "Open the east window"; and he opened it. Then Elisha said, "Shoot"; and he shot. And he said, "The arrow of the Lord's deliverance…from Syria; for you must strike the Syrians at Aphek till you have destroyed them." Then he said, "Take the arrows"; so he took them. And he said to the king of Israel, "Strike the ground"; so he struck three times, and stopped. And the man of God was angry with him, and said, "You should have struck five or six times; then you would have struck Syria till you had destroyed it! But now you will strike Syria only three times." (2 Kings 13:14–19)

Nobody told the king how many times to strike the ground. That was his choice. Nobody told him how to strike the arrows on the ground. That was his choice. But the way he did it and the lack of intensity with which he did it showed the prophet of God what kind of king he was dealing with—he saw that the king had no heart to smite the Syrians. The prophet wanted the king to grab those arrows and smite the ground with blood in his eyes.

GROWTH INSIGHT

Hit It! (Finish Strong!)
Hit It! (Finish Strong!)
Hit It! (Finish Strong!)
Hit It! (Finish Strong!)
Hit It! (Finish Strong!)
Hit It! (Finish Strong!)

Give a serving to seven, and also to eight, for you do not know what evil will be on the earth. (Ecclesiastes 11:2)

This Scripture teaches us to be generous and strong in all that we do. The "evil that will be on the earth" speaks of times of hardship when you need to be sure of your salvation and strong in your decisions.

GROWTH INSIGHT

If you do what's right today it will be enough for tomorrow.

Now that you have completed this thirty-one day series on growing up, you need to ask yourself the right questions:

- What kind of heart do I have?

- What kind of disciplines am I developing in my life?

- How am I equipping myself to go the distance and finish strong?

How you answer these questions will determine how tall you become on the inside and how you will finish this race.

GROWTH INSIGHT

You've got to *take* what you have
and *use* what you have,
with *all* that you have,
to finish the race with maturity and passion.

ABOUT THE AUTHOR

D r. Randy Bozarth and his wife, Susan, have planted four churches, as well as filling in as interim pastors of several churches that were going though leadership change.

In 1992, after establishing a local church on Hilton Head Island, South Carolina, they sensed a strong witness to move out into full-time missions ministry. Dr. Bozarth joined the staff of Christ For The Nations located in Dallas, Texas. Randy served Christ For The Nations for thirteen years in various capacities.

His responsibilities included providing spiritual and academic accountability to more than forty Christ For The Nations affiliated schools around the world, representing more than 3,000 students. Dr. Bozarth served as vice president of CFNI for eight years.

In 1997, Dr. Bozarth was instrumental in the founding of Christ For The Nations Church. He also managed the CFN Archives to preserve the Pentecostal heritage of the organization.

In the past ten years, Dr. Bozarth has ministered in more than forty nations. His focus on teaching and ministry is Christian maturity, leadership, and strengthening the body of Christ. He encourages believers to cultivate a passion for the empowering of the Holy Spirit in their daily lives.

Dr. Bozarth is a dynamic motivational speaker, consultant to national and international leaders and an author of four books, *The Voice of Healing, A Voice That Still Speaks, The Demon of Self-Deception, Your Mouth Is Killing You,* and the latest, *31 Days of Spiritual Growth: Discover Your Passionate Purpose. The Demon of Self-Deception* has also been published in Spanish.

Presently, Dr. Bozarth is founder and president of World Missions Advance, a missions organization that brings strength and support to missionaries around the world.

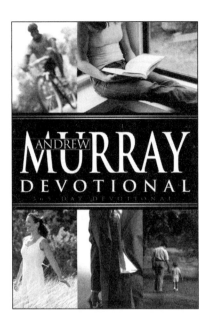

Andrew Murray Devotional
Andrew Murray

Andrew Murray's uplifting messages for each day of the
year will comfort and refresh you in your walk with God.
Spending time with God daily will bring a new joy and peace
into your life. As you daily explore these truths from Andrew
Murray, you will connect with God's glorious power and
see impossibilities turn into realities. Your prayer life will be
transformed. You will experience the joy of seeing powerful
results in your life as you minister to others. Don't miss out
on the most important part of the day—your miraculous,
life-changing moments spent with the Creator.

ISBN: 978-0-88368-778-9 • Trade • 400 pages

www.whitakerhouse.com